THE DANAHER
DIARIES VOL. II

100 More of John Danaher's Musings on
Learning, Teaching, Strategy, and Mastery

It is natural to think that justice would decree that the skills you worked so hard to develop in the dojo would stay unblemished with you for a lifetime once you gained them - given that ownership came at such a steep price in sweat and effort. This is an illusion. Of all the things you own - your skills are the most perishable. Against an opponent of similar skill and experience - you are only as good as the last one hundred and fifty days of your training. Gaining skills is only the first battle - keeping them is a much longer and lonelier one.

The world of jiu-jitsu is undergoing a sea change. While so many martial arts see their chief aim as preserving history, Brazilian jiu-jitsu has always been rooted in the idea of finding new innovations to defeat old ideas. Our history is one of questioning, experimenting, modifying, and ultimately testing new ideas on the battlefield. The jiu-jitsu that emerged from Brazil has never been academic. Real fighters, really employing its techniques, sometimes for life and death. That may be the only history that matters.

Today, the stakes may seem lower. The samurai are gone and the days of vale tudo have given way to a golden age of competitive grappling. A dozen different formats, rulesets, and champions. But the heart and soul of jiu-jitsu is unchanged: a group of fighters looking for that edge. Just as generals of old looked for new technology to win wars, our technology is our minds and our army is our body. Whomever can see and old idea in a new light, can be tomorrow's champion.

Or even better, can create champions.

For more than a decade, John Danaher was the silent Kingmaker. With no academy or branding of his own, the Renzo Gracie black belt quietly built a stable of mixed martial arts and submission grappling phenoms. But after the breakthrough success of George St. Pierre, Danaher was forced to surrender his relative anonymity. In the early 2010's, Danaher turned his focus to submission grappling, intrigued by the new wave of interest in nogi competition. His ranks swelled, and his mystique grew. While many coaches have produced champions, Danaher seemed to be making more of them, with consistency. What's more, he was able to do so largely off his spoken word alone. John himself was not an active competitor, and never had been. In fact, at different times in his career injuries had prevented him from training at all. When outsiders asked what the secret weapon was, Danaher's students never cited harder-than-hell training or the cutting edge strength and conditioning program. They attributed it to one thing:

This guy is a genius.

For a long time, the world was left to theorize on what exactly that meant. At first, it seemed largely due to Danaher's pro team having an early mastery of the leg control positions. It was their technological edge in the early parts of the decade. But as the rest of the world caught up with the once dismissed art of ashi garame, the now infamous "Danaher Death Squad" did not fall by the wayside. They continued to thrive and adapt to the changing tides of submission grappling. With Danaher's somewhat secluded "blue basement" and evasive personality, the world was left to wonder just what this system was that Danaher was teaching and how he was always one step ahead of the next trend.

Then Instagram happened.

Piece by piece and day by day, the musings of Danaher on social media took form as he riffed on his ideas of kaizen, control, entanglements, and the keys to improving in jiu-jitsu. As his post count inched up week after week, his thought process seemed to come into focus. Jiu-jitsu was a game of concepts, rules, maxims, and metaphors. The one who could organize and communicate them best as a unified theory, would produce the best students.

And while his thoughts on social media may be disjointed, there are enough of them now that they *can* be codified and organized in such a way that his system can be understood. At the very least, plenty can be gleamed from it.

The first Danaher Diaries was a surprise hit, but the journey never ends. As John himself has said, you're only as good as your recent training. And while it may seem like John could only have so much to say, sometimes we need to hear things said many different ways. Why else would world champions like Gary Tonon and Gordon Ryan continue to show up in the Blue Basement day after day? Even *their* skills are perishable.

So wherever you are now, sitting in your car before the gym opens, in a quiet moment with your morning coffee, or in the final moments before a good night's rest. Get ready to bow in.

Class is about to start.

GUARD RETENTION: One of the most exciting aspects of learning Jiu Jitsu is that of developing strong attacks with submissions and sweeps/reversals from bottom guard positions. Most people believe that in any combat situation a person in top position will have an advantage over an opponent underneath them. It is very eye opening to a beginner to see how powerful certain bottom guard positions can be if used well. However, EVEN THE BEST ATTACKING ABILITIES FROM BOTTOM POSITION WILL BE OF LITTLE VALUE IF YOU CANNOT MAINTAIN A GUARD POSITION LONG ENOUGH TO ACTUALLY PUT THEM INTO OPERATION. The bottom game of Jiu Jitsu is entirely predicated on the idea that you must be able to engage your opponent with your LEGS (Guard) If you are to be effective. If your opponent quickly passes your legs, you can't do anything from underneath until you recover your legs back between yourself and your adversary. If you have connection of your legs to your opponent or least alignment of your legs with your opponent, you can play an offensive game from bottom, but the moment he passes your guard, you are 100% defensive. As such, the ability to hold a guard position for extended periods of time against resistance is the single most important skill in building a foundation for offense from bottom position. While it may not have the sex appeal of submissions and sweeps, you won't be submitting or sweeping anyone from underneath if they pass your legs - so when it comes to developing bottom guard skills - EVERYTHING STARTS WITH RETENTION. Only when you have that skill will you be able to constantly attack and play an offensive game from bottom position. AS LONG AS YOU HAVE YOUR LEGS/ HIPS POSITIONED BETWEEN YOURSELF AND YOUR OPPONENT YOU ARE A THREAT TO HIM - AS SOON AS HE PASSES YOUR GUARD YOU ARE NOTHING TO HIM BUT A TARGET. Work hard on those unglamorous but essential retention skills - they will provide more value to your bottom game than any other and create a foundation upon which you can build a truly impressive set of bottom offense skills

TWO DIFFERENT APPROACHES TO SUBMISSION: I have always taught Jiu Jitsu as the art and science of control that leads to submission. When it is time to enter submissions, understand that there are two general methods. The first is to emphasize SPEED OF ENTRY. The idea is to catch your opponent in a moment of vulnerability PRIOR TO HIS ABILITY TO SET UP STRONG DEFENSES. The second is to get to a completed dominant position first, your opponent recognizes the danger of the position and sets up strong defensive apparatus in response to the threat, and you employ a STEP BY STEP DISMANTLING OF HIS DEFENSES TO GET THE BREAKTHROUGH. The first relies upon your ability to sense OPPORTUNITY and have the speed to get to the prize before your opponent can construct defenses. The second relies upon your KNOWLEDGE OF THE MAJOR COUNTERS TO YOUR THREAT AND YOUR ABILITY TO OVERCOME THEM. If you wish to maximize your potential in the use of submission holds - you must gain expertise in both methods. The dynamic nature of sparring and competition will provide you with many opportunities to use the first method and snatch submissions in the midst of the action. As you develop strong positional skills you will get opportunities to also employ the second approach. Note that the first approach relies mostly upon your PERCEPTION. YOU MUST TRAIN YOURSELF TO SEE OPPORTUNITY AND ACT IMMEDIATELY UPON IT. The second relies more upon knowledge of PROCEDURE and a methodical dismantling of defensive structures. The best students are always those who can double their chances by using both with equal efficacy. Play them both and watch your submission game take a jump forward!

WHEN STRANGLEHOLDS AND JOINT LOCKS JOIN
FORCES: The submission holds of Jiu Jitsu are
broadly divided into JOINT LOCKS and
STRANGLES. The former is an attack upon your
opponent's body, the latter an attack upon your
opponent's consciousness. Both are devastating
weapons. There are a few occasions when you
can bridge the divide and make them work
together as one. Arguably the best example of
this is the triangle (sankaku). Anytime you lock
up a triangle of any type upon an opponent you
always have the option of adding a lock to your
opponent's wrist, elbow or shoulder as well. The
effects of this can be devastating as typically the
defenses to the strangle tend to open you up to
the joint locks and vice versa, so that the
opponent is given the devils choice between
getting strangled vs getting broken. Look for this
every time you attack with triangles of all types
and begin to exploit the potential of both
strangles and joint locks at the same time!

THE IRON LAW OF SPEED VS CONTROL: When we go to engage with an opponent, a basic choice we must make is THE SPEED OF OUR OWN MOVEMENT vs THE CONTROL WE HAVE OVER OUR OPPONENTS MOVEMENT. There is an iron rule that comes into play here that has deep ramifications for our game. You must make a choice between speed and control - You cannot have both at the same time. The more you emphasize the speed of your own movements the less you will be able to control the movements of your opponent. Since Jiu Jitsu is a sport that primarily emphasize control above all else - it is typically a slow-paced game in comparison to other grappling sports such as wrestling and judo. Note that all the fastest moves of Jiu Jitsu, for example a flying arm bar, are among the least controlling and need speed and surprise to get the win before our opponent can react defensively. The slowest moves of Jiu Jitsu - the dominant pins - where minutes can go by with very little movement are the most controlling. This iron law of speed and control is something you must ponder when building your own game. Both can be highly successful. It is also quite possible to use both at different times and in different contexts. For example, standing position is inherently less controlling than ground positions and thus speed plays a much greater role in success for most athletes. You might play a speed-based game standing but a control-based game on the floor. Both speed and control are wonderful attributes for combat athletes to develop - but learning to understand their relationship and how that relationship will impact your game is a big part of your Jiu Jitsu journey.

KNOWING WHAT YOU ARE FIGHTING AGAINST IS HALF THE BATTLE - GUARD RETENTION: There are few skills in Jiu Jitsu that are more important for success than guard retention. If someone passes your guard, you are now one hundred percent defensive and you won't be able to get back on the offense until you recover your guard. In a short time limit match, this may mean that half the match time is lost based on that one mistake. Moreover, now your opponent is ahead on points and no longer feels compelled to engage. Consequently, you will have to push the action to catch up - never easy on an opponent who is not engaging. Guard retention is among the more difficult skills to teach to students. I always like to begin by clearly outlining what an opponent actually has to do to pass your guard. In fact, it is not an easy process. He must complete five sequential steps

1 - Break whatever grip/connection you have to him sufficiently to be able to move independently of you

2 - get an angle

3 - close distance and bypass your legs and get past the line of your hips

4 - lower his level to get chest to chest (or in some cases knee to stomach)

5 - hold you in a pin with one shoulder to the floor for three seconds That's a lot of work! Your job as the athlete retaining guard is to fight each one of those sequential steps as they occur. THE FURTHER INTO THE SEQUENCE YOUR OPPONENT GETS THE MORE DIFFICULT THE TASK OF RETENTION BECOMES AND THE MORE RISK YOU WILL HAVE TO TAKE TO PREVENT THE PASS. By breaking down the act of passing into these sequential steps, students can more easily identify what they must do to stop an opponent and when they ought to be applying a given defense. Once your retention game has a sense of DIRECTION you can take away the mad scramble elements that often detract from many beginning athletes attempts at guard retention and skillfully hold off even a determined passer - and when you can HOLD a

guard, you can ATTACK and FINISH from guard - and that's what Jiu Jitsu bottom position is all about!

GETTING IT RIGHT: The sport of Jiu Jitsu is one of the most technically demanding in all of sports. A submission that was 99% correct fails as badly as one that was 5% correct. There is a lot of heartache over moves that got close - but failed. Interestingly, the cause of failure is usually something very small. That is why such a premium is put upon small technical details in Jiu Jitsu because they are the difference between almost winning (but losing) and winning. IN A SKILL WHERE THERE IS ONLY SUCCESS AND FAILURE AND ANYTHING LESS THAT COMPLETE SUCCESS IS FAILURE - EVERYTHING DOWN TO THE SMALLEST DETAILS HAS TO BE CORRECT. The number of high percentage submissions in Jiu Jitsu is small - I really only focus on twenty, and most of my time is spent on only six systems of submissions which form the core of our arsenal - the course of your study must focus on the DEPTH of your knowledge of a few moves. So, work hard to amass those match winning details. When a fleeting opportunity arises before you against a tough opponent, they will be the difference between triumph and frustration

THE FOUNDATION OF YOUR GAME: The essential nature of Jiu Jitsu is that it is built around the idea that your first responsibility is to REMOVE THE DANGER OF THE WORST CASE SCENARIO. The worst-case scenario is always that of an opponent getting past your legs and into superior upper body pins from where he can pick and choose his attacks whilst you can do nothing in return. As such, the foundation of your Jiu Jitsu journey must always be the two skills of GETTING OUT OF PINS and STOPPING SOMEONE GETTING PAST YOUR LEGS AND PINNING YOU. Thus, it is the skills of PIN ESCAPES and GUARD RETENTION that you must master first. Without these prerequisites all the other skills of Jiu Jitsu are of little practical value. You may have a fine arm bar or triangle, but if your opponent brushes past your guard and pins you, you'll simply never get a chance to use it. Even worse, if you know you struggle to get out of pins or your guard is easy to pass, you will stop YOURSELF from using your arm bar and triangle for fear of the risk of getting pinned if it does not work. So, whenever beginner students or students with a confidence issue (afraid to pull the trigger when opportunity presents itself) come to me for advice on what they should focus on first, my answer is almost always - PIN ESCAPES and GUARD RETENTION. These two skills will be the foundation upon which you can build a game that can take you far. Without them the best you will achieve is a hit and miss Jiu Jitsu and as your opponent's get better - far more misses than hits. If they can't pass your guard you will always be capable of offense from bottom position. Ironically it is your defensive skills that will determine the reach and extent of your offensive skills. Take pride in being UNPINNABLE and UNPASSABLE (impassable) - only then will you be able to achieve your final goal of attacks that are UNSTOPPABLE

THE BATTLE FOR SPACE: In Jiu Jitsu the aims/goals of the top athlete are usually diametrically opposed to this of the bottom athlete. The goal of the athlete in top position is typically to CLOSE DISTANCE, GET TIGHT TO HIS OPPONENT AND RESTRICT SPACE. There is a reason for this. Almost all the bottom moves of Jiu Jitsu require some amount of space between you and your opponent to work - take away that space and you shut the bottom man down into a totally defensive game. The athlete on bottom wants the opposite - he must constantly fight to CREATE AND MAINTAIN SPACE so that he can play effective offense from underneath. The number one weapon for the bottom athlete is this war over space is the use of FRAMES - positioning your limbs as braces to hold an opponent at distance long enough to thwart his attempts to smother and pin you. Understanding and implementing the constant battle between the bottom athletes attempts to use frames and the top athletes attempts to negate them is a big part of your development. Your ability to improvise frames with your hands, forearms, elbows and your ability to combine these with appropriate body movements are the basis of one of the most crucial skills in the sport - GUARD RETENTION. The interplay between your ability to FRAME WITH YOUR ARMS and RECOVER WITH YOUR LEGS will determine your ability to retain guard and an aggressive passer. The outcome of this battle will almost always determine the outcome of the battle overall.

CLIMB - DON'T JUMP: When we go to engage our opponent, we must have a goal in mind - usually it is one of our favorite attacking positions. Now you don't get given your favorite attacking positions for free - you must EARN them. Often, I see people trying to jump immediately to their favorite grips/positions. This can work on occasion, especially against opponents who don't know your game and who you can thus surprise. However, once your tricks are shown and the surprise lost, you won't get there anymore. The best way to get to your favorite attacking positions is to CLIMB THE BODY AND WORK YOUR WAY REMORSELESSLY TOWARDS THEM. Start with the part of your opponent's body that is closest to you - usually his hands/wrists - and work up the arms to the torso/legs. The general pattern is that YOU START WITH THE EXTREMITIES AND WORK YOUR WAY TO THE CENTER OF MASS/TORSO. Avoid skipping steps especially when the opponent is skilled. CLIMB HIS BODY AS YOU

WOULD A ROPE - WE DON'T JUMP TO THE TOP OF THE ROPE BUT CLIMB HAND BY HAND TO THE TOP. This approach will give you great connection and control - the hallmarks of good Jiu Jitsu. Make it your modus operandi and watch your performance improve!

THE MAGIC OF CROSS COLLAR GRIPS: In all aspects of Jiu Jitsu - THE BEGINNING OF CONTROL IS GRIP. When you go to grip an opponent, you have a vast array of options, particularly when using the gi. Understand that each of the major grips offers a different type of control. Arguably the most important form of control is HEAD CONTROL. This is due to the basic nature of the human body. We humans are essentially a skull connected to a spine and everything hangs off that - so if you control the head - you control everything else by default. The gi is a rope around your opponent's neck and offers a tremendous degree of indirect head control. As such, you want to take advantage of it as much as possible. When you first begin your Jiu jitsu journey I often recommend to use the cross lapel grip as your DEFAULT GRIP in most neutral positions on the ground (in standing situations straight collar grips are usually preferred) - if you are ever unsure where or how to grip in neutral positions, just go cross collar and in the majority of cases it will work well. As you gain in gripping expertise you will learn that gripping higher or lower can have important effects and that strangulation can be added to control. Take time to study the incredible potential of this foundational grip - it's value will extend throughout your entire time in jiujitsu.

ORIENTATION: Our goal is always control that leads to submission. Once you get a submission hold locked on, the defensive reactions from your opponent can be very strong indeed - after all, nobody wants to be the guy that tapped out. One of the more common defensive reactions to some of the major submission holds are turning or spinning escapes. These have an immediate effect - you will have to follow an opponent through three hundred and sixty degrees of rotation (sometimes several times) and STILL BE ABLE TO ACHIEVE THE BREAK OF STRANGLE AT ANY TIME DURING THAT ROTATION. As such, you must train yourself to be able to finish REGARDLESS OF THE ORIENTATION YOU FIND YOURSELF IN. We usually train our submission holds only in conventional or standard orientations, but the reality is that in a competitive match you will have to finish in many unconventional orientations. For all your favorite submissions make your You practice your finishes through a full three hundred and sixty degrees so that you don't have any surprises when it's time to finish upside down or back to front in a match.

EACH OF THE MAIN MOVES OF JIU JITSU HAS ITS OWN
SPECIAL CHARACTER - learn to understand that
character and you will go far: There is no
question that certain moves in Jiu Jitsu have
prominence among the countless moves of the
sport. Some are what we often call "high
percentage" That is, they work repeatedly across
all body types, personalities, weight categories,
ages, both sexes, at all belt levels. So, for
example, in every tournament you will see
examples of high percentage moves such as
single leg, double leg, elbow escape, guillotines,
juji gatame arm bar, triangles, Kimura etc. These
high percentage moves must be the basis of your
game. Understand that all these moves have
their own character. They are strong in some
ways, weak in others. They have good points and
bad points. Developing a deep relationship with
each of these moves is a huge part of your Jiu
Jitsu journey. Just as you have your favorite
friends and you understand the character of
each very well, so that you have a friend who

you know is probably not the best one to bring with you to the museum, but is your go too back up in a bar brawl, another who is rather boring but perfect as a study partner before a big exam etc. you associate each friend with an appropriate context and they can help you through life - so too with your Jiu Jitsu moves. Each will do well and help you in a certain context and poorly in others. Your job is to understand the moves so well that you know not only the move - BUT THE CONTEXT IN WHICH TO APPLY THEM. Know your favorite moves as intimately as your closest friends, understand their good and bad points and they will never let you down

VARYING YOUR INTENSITY LEVELS: A truly vital skill in grappling is that of learning to VARY YOUR LEVELS OF PHYSICAL INTENSITY ACCORDING TO THE DEMANDS OF THE SITUATION YOU ARE IN. Probably the single most common problem I see in beginning students is an inability to change and regulate the intensity of their physical effort - they just go at maximum intensity the whole match. The inevitable result is that that quickly tire and fade. The other extreme is athletes who play so loose that when it's time to pull the trigger and hit a move, are so loose that it is simply ineffective. Somewhere in between these extremes is the happy medium you seek. As a general price of advice - only employ maximal muscle contractions in short bursts and only when actually looking to perform a given move. At other times stay in a state of relaxed focus. Not that even in those short bursts of maximal muscular exertion - KEEP BREATHING and don't use muscular strength to compensate for positional errors -

get your body in good position first and THEN apply your strength. In this way you can play a hard-physical game without exhausting yourself to a point where you become ineffective. Look at this picture. Georges St-Pierre has gotten into a potential finishing position and is thus ready to apply some serious force - the strain shows. Next to him Gordon Ryan has gotten to a dominant position but does not yet have a finishing hold in place and so takes on a very relaxed demeanor. The contrast between them is striking and instructive - one situation demands muscular tension and exertion, the other allows relaxation on the understanding that this will preserve your strength for a time when it is needed. KEEP MONITORING YOU STRENGTH/TENSION OUTPUT AS YOU ENGAGE YOUR OPPONENT. Know when to be tight and when to be loose and you will defeat many opponents on endurance alone and the rest by having the physicality in reserve to finish that potential match winning move.

DAYLIGHT: The main means by which we immobilize opponents in Jiu Jitsu is to place wedges around their body and reinforce these wedges with weight (if we are on top) locked limbs (closed wedges) or muscular tension. A big factor in how effective these immobilizing wedges will be is the degree of connection between them and your opponent. The saying I always use is this - IF YOU CAN SEE DAYLIGHT BETWEEN YOUR WEDGES AND HIS BODY - YOU ARE MAKING HIS ESCAPE EASY. Whenever you go to lock an opponent down - look for daylight (space) around your limbs and his body. Try always to fit your body tightly into his - space is your enemy here. Make your body initially soft and flexible so that you can contour your body around his and there is no daylight between you and him. Then when it is time to apply to move puts tension through your body long enough to get the job done. This is an easy thing for a camera to reveal or a friend to see - often you can see it in yourself from your own perspective

- WHENEVER YOU SEE IT - ELIMINATE IT - because it is the downfall of many an attempted move.

DIRECTION OF FORCE: Every move in Jiu Jitsu requires the application of force. The single biggest determinant of how successful that application of force will be is the DIRECTION you apply the force. SMALLER FORCES APPLIED IN THE APPROPRIATE DIRECTION WILL ALWAYS OUTPERFORM BIGGER FORCES APPLIED IN FAULTY DIRECTIONS. For all your favorite moves, study the optimal directions to apply forces when performing those moves. Understand that those directions can change mid-move and you may well have to adjust on the fly. Knowing the difference between sound and unsound direction of force will often make the difference between success and failure. Next time on the mat you feel your application of force get stopped by a tough opponent - EXPERIMENT WITH CHANGES IN DIRECTION - sometimes even a small change will make a big difference. When you do you will have taken a big step towards the Jiu Jitsu ideal of GETTING MORE DONE WITH LESS EFFORT.

WHEN ATTACKING WITH ASHI GARAMI - make your first movement hip to hip: The single most common cause of failure for all submission attacks is too much space between the points of connection between your body and your opponent's - leg locking from ashi garami is no exception. I always counsel my students when attacking with ashi garami based leg locks - make your first movement a scoot of your hips to your opponent's hips - everything else comes after this. NO OTHER ADJUSTMENT OR COMPENSATION YOU CAN MAKE CAN ATONE FOR FAILURE TO CLOSE DISTANCE AND CONNECT PROPERLY - so make that your priority. This makes all subsequent actions towards a break easier and more efficient - resulting in a perfect lock and victory.

WHEN WORKING ARM BARS FROM UNDERNEATH A
STRONGLY RESISTING OPPONENT - get your hips
pointing in the same direction your opponent is
facing: The juji gatame arm bar from guard is
among the most popular and effective moves in
the sport. Using it well is very instructive for
many other skills as well. An important general
principle in combat sports is to avoid head to
head confrontations that pit your strength
directly against that of an opponent - this
approach will never allow you to defeat
stronger opponents. The idea is to seek to align
your forces with his as much as possible so that
you DEFLECT and REDIRECT force rather than
CONFRONT IT HEAD ON. In the case of the
classic arm bar from guard, a good way to
ensure you do this is to go beyond a ninety-
degree pivot when in the arm bar position. Get
your hips pointing forward in the same
direction your opponent is facing (or at least as
close as you can). In this way your legs and hips
will push in the same direction as your

opponent's defensive downward/forward stacking force. This addition of your force to his will enable you to easily off balance him from bottom. An opponent out of balance is easily attacked and finished or toppled over into a more compromised position from where you can renew the attack. Whenever you find your arm bar attack from guard stopped by your opponent's defensive reaction - TAKE THE EXTRA TIME TO LINE UP YOUR HIPS WITH HIS DIRECTION AND APPLY THE FORCE OF YOUR LEGS IN CONCERT WITH HIS. Your success rate will greatly increase, and his defensive reaction will aid you rather than stop you.

IF YOU LOOK AT ALL THE CHAMPIONS OF JIU JITSU FOR THE LAST TWENTY-FIVE YEARS - a clear idea emerges - NO ONE BODY TYPE OR PERSONALITY TYPE DOMINATES THE SPORT. You see tremendous variation among the champions. The beauty of Jiu Jitsu and indeed, all combat sports is that they allow every one of us regardless of our physical or psychological type to find our own path to excellence. I have seen tall, short, thick and thin athletes become champions. I have seen both the nervous and the fearless, the confident and the anxiety ridden get to the top. Your job is to find one path among the myriad options that Jiu Jitsu offers that works for you - if you can and you can work hard to master it, you can achieve great things apply force second: One of the most common mistakes I see among developing grapplers is a tendency to get the opportunity for a submission and jump in with maximum force as soon as they enter the submission hold. This usually results in large amounts of energy expenditure and is a quick route to exhaustion and frustration. Take a little time to set your immobilizing wedges and your breaking fulcrums and make sure to seize the longest lever you can and only then apply your force. You will immediately see results. The submission holds of Jiu Jitsu are devastating when properly set, but feeble when poorly set. Get it right first - then your application of force will almost always get the results you seek. Remember that with submission holds it's not how fast you get there that counts, but rather, what effects you can generate ONCE you get there. So, give yourself a little time to adjust, a little time to refine and you will generate a LOT more force through the proper use of lever and fulcrum than you ever could through muscular exertion.

YOU CAN'T CLOSE ALL THE DOORS… and neither can your opponent: A big part of what makes Jiu Jitsu so fascinating, so frustrating and so uplifting; is the fact that our job is to shut down our opponent's ability to move - TO CLOSE ALL THE DOORWAYS TO ESCAPE SO TO SAY. So, if an opponent is using an under hook to escape, we can close that door by pummeling in our own under hook. If he is turning his head inwards to begin an elbow escape we might close that door with a strong cross face - and so it goes on - the better we get at Jiu Jitsu, the better we get and closing off all the routes to escape - closing each door as our opponent tries to open them. Understand however, that you can only shut so many doors at once - YOU CAN NEVER SHUT THEM ALL SIMULTANEOUSLY. As you focus on shutting down one area, ANOTHER DOOR MUST OPEN SOMEWHERE ELSE. This means that NO MEANS OF CONTROL IN JIU JITSU CAN EVER BE COMPLETE. The ramifications of this are deep. It means first, that we must move on from control and actual FINISH opponents, because you can never hold a skilled opponent for ever as eventually, they will find an open door. Second, if you are the one being controlled, NEVER LOSE HOPE. There is an open door there somewhere no matter how hopeless the situation might seem - you just have to find it. This simple insight of the impossibility of closing all the doors of escape is both a source of frustration and hope. Frustration because you can never completely shut down an opponent's ability to escape your control (and so the onus is on you to go forward without delay to the finish). Hope, because no matter how shackled you might feel, you always know that somewhere there is an open door for you to walk through.

WE ALL HAVE OUR FAVORITES: A huge part of your progress comes from acquiring and developing your FAVORITE MOVES (tokui-waza). These are the moves that suite your body type and personality more than any others and with which you show early promise. Remember you are involved in a sport where A PERFECT APPLICATION OF ONE MOVE WILL WIN A MATCH, BUT THE IMPERFECT APPLICATION OF A HUNDRED MOVES WON'T DO A DAMN THING. When you acquire some favorites that seem to work for you - preferably high percentage moves - DEVOTE A BIG PART OF YOUR TRAINING TIME TO ENLARGE AND PERFECT YOUR UNDERSTANDING AND PERFORMANCE OF THISE MOVES. How good you get at those favorite moves will determine how good you get at the sport overall. Only once you have some heavy hitting main weapons can you branch off those main attacks to add new directions to your game. Let your opponent react to your main weapons and defeat him on his reactions to the strong initial threat - that is the pattern of good Jiu Jitsu for most people.

STEP OUTSIDE OF YOURSELF AND OBSERVE YOUR
GAME: One of the most factors in your progress
in Jiu Jitsu is SELF KNOWLEDGE. If you can make
an honest and accurate assessment of your
current skill set then you can plan accurately
what you need to improve and add to it to
become the athlete you want to be. It is difficult
to this, especially when you first begin the sport
- you simply don't have the knowledge yet to
accurately assess your level and what else needs
to be learned. In time however, you will learn
the skill of SELF ASSESSMENT. Let me tell you
that this skill is crucial for your progress. One of
my primary functions as a coach is to ASSESS MY
ATHLETES AND MAKE DECISIONS WHAT THEY
NEED TO CHANGE TO GET TO IMPROVE THEIR
PERFORMANCE. If you have an outside pair of
eyes to do this for you - wonderful - it will be a
great benefit. If you don't - you will have to learn
to do it yourself. Start writing down the things
you believe you do well against your peers.
Compare this with a list of things you think

would make you perform better and write down the reasons WHY you think those additions are well suited to you as an individual and will be good additions to your current skill set. Now write down the skills you think are necessary but which you perform poorly. Compare and contrast the lists of skills that you do well and those which you perform poorly. What is the correlation between the two? Searching yourself in this way can teach you a lot about yourself and your current game - and the more you know about that, THE MORE YOU CAN MAKE BENEFICIAL CHANGES. Keep an eye on the game, keep an eye on your role models - but don't forget to keep an eye on yourself...

Imagine you knew literally nothing about punching. You found a competent boxing coach and in your first lesson he taught you one punch - a basic jab to the head. At the end of your first class you are excited to have a little knowledge of one punch. In your second class he teaches you another punch - a straight rear hand to the head. Now you are pleased to know a little about two punches. On your way home you reflect on your progress and wonder how many punching attacks you could use on an opponent. You know TWO punches, but you can throw FOUR attacks off just this tiny amount of knowledge you have. You know two moves - jab and rear straight - but you can use them in four ways - jab, rear straight, jab followed by rear straight and rear straight followed by jab. So, you in your second class you DOUBLED the number of punches you knew but QUADRUPLED the number of different blows you could throw by doing so. THIS IS THE

MAGIC OF COMBINATION ATTACKS IN A NUTSHELL. Even a small number of moves can be worked together in combinations to create limitless combinations that opponents will find extremely difficult to stop. Now add a few more moves, double jab, jab to the body, rear straight to the body - and suddenly the number of different striking attacks rises EXPONENTIALLY as the combinations of a few similar moves creates massive numbers of potential attacks that even very skilled opponents will really struggle to keep up with. EXACTLY THE SAME LESSON APPLIES TO GRAPPLING. My students have some the highest finishing rates in Jiu Jitsu, yet Ninety percent of our finishes come from combining just six submissions holds. You must learn to make the incredible potential power of COMBINED ATTACKS work in your favor. Don't just drill and spar with single attacks in mind but always ask what will be your follow up if this should prove insufficient - start with it as a mental habit and then it will become a physical habit that will greatly improve your success rates.

INDIRECT ATTACKS: When you first begin studying Jiu Jitsu you learn your first basic attacks - an arm bar from guard, a strangle from the back, a guillotine etc. In beginners' class you see an opportunity and you try to apply the move. You do DIRECTLY to the move from observing the opportunity. As your opponent's learn the same moves you are learning, they soon learn the warning signs that you are entering into a move and they start reacting defensively to frustrate you. Because you are going directly to the move, this is easy for them to do. This is when the great law of KNOWLEDGE AND ATTACK comes into play. THE MORE DEFENSIVE KNOWLEDGE AND SKILL YOUR OPPONENT POSSESSES, THE MORE YOU MUST EMPLOY INDIRECT ATTACKS TO DISGUISE YOUR REAL INTENTIONS TO A KNOWLEDGEABLE OPPONENT AND BREAK THROUGH THEIR DEFENSE VIA MISDIRECTION. You must learn to get your opponent reacting to false attacks/direction in order to break through with real attacks. THE

LESS SOPHISTICATED YOUR OPPONENT - THE MORE DIRECT YOUR ATTACKS OUGHT TO BE. THE MORE SOPHISTICATED YOUR OPPONENT, THE MORE INDIRECT YOUR ATTACKS SHOULD BE. So if I am attacking someone with great lower body defense and I want the right leg, I may well fake an attack to the neck, as he reacts to the fake, go into another fake attack to the left arm, as an the opponent skillfully reacts to this, enter into the REAL attack on the right leg that I wanted all along. Moving in this way I am much more likely to break through sophisticated defenses than simple direct attacks. Making a habit of housing your favorite attacks in the context of INDIRECT approaches will greatly raise your success rate against talented opponents

DRILLING AS AN IDEAL: We spend a lot of time drilling - there is a simple question that fascinates me - IS IT WORTH IT? Is it possible that we would be better off just sparring the entire workout instead? I usually have about 1/2 - 2/3 of my workouts as drilling and 1/2 - 1/3 sparring - is it possible that all that is a waste of time and we would be better off just 100% sparring? I have many reasons why I am a strong advocate of drilling as an essential part of a daily Jiu Jitsu workout and why I believe it translates into faster progress for most (not all) students. One of the simplest is the argument that WE ALL NEED AN IDEAL TOWARDS WHICH WE AIM OURSELVES. If we have a strong mental ideal IT CAN HELP PULL OUR PHYSICAL BODY CLOSER TO THAT MENTAL IDEAL - EVEN IF WE NEVER REACH IT. We all know that in most cases we look a lot smoother and more competent when we drill a move on a cooperative training partner than we ever do in a live sparring situation against a competitive opponent. Drills let us get close to the IDEAL of what we OUGHT to look and feel like when we perform a given move - an elusive ideal to strive for. We know very well it won't look that smooth and clean in a competitive match - BUT THE HIGHER OUR STANDARDS IN DRILLING, THE HIGHER OUR PERFORMANCE IN A MATCH. This is one of many reasons why I favor drills as a substantial part of your overall training time - the ratio may change depending on circumstances sometimes drills are only 1/4 of the workout, but always they are there. I do believe that different people need different ratios and that there are some who do better almost exclusively with sparring and for whom drilling does little good; but for the vast majority drilling technique in some way (obviously there are many types of drills) is a key part of faster progress.

KEEP YOUR BODY WARM, YOUR MIND CALCULATING AND YOUR HEART COLD: Everyone has their own mental approach to Jiu Jitsu and in truth I have seen great champions with every possible mindset from extreme fear to extreme confidence - so I don't believe it's possible to say there is any one correct way to mentally enter a match. I will say this however, if your inclination is, as mine is, to see Jiu Jitsu as first and foremost a game of knowledge and decisions and problem solving - then I recommend keeping yourself in an emotionally neutral and cold-blooded state. Why? Because we do our calculations and problem solving best in a psychologically calm state. Imagine trying to solve a complex math problem whilst angry and agitated and you will get a sense of what I mean. Better to wait an hour, calm down and focus and then solve the problem. So, if you favor a knowledge based/problem solving approach to Jiu Jitsu, train yourself to work in a state of relative calm. If you prefer a more intuitive, combative approach, it may well be better to go in hot blooded - champions have arisen from both - but know your own game and base your mental preparation upon that.

WHEN THE ACTION STARTS - HAVE A PLAN OF ATTACK: It is very difficult to impose yourself upon the outcomes if you simply drift into the action when sparring starts. While you can never predict the entirety of any given match - YOU CAN ALMOST ALWAYS PREDICT THE OPENING SEQUENCES OF A MATCH BASED UPON YOUR RESPECTIVE STANCES AND MOTION. What happens in those opening sequences will often have real effects for the duration of the match - so impose yourself in the opening exchanges - KNOW WHAT YOU WANT AND HAVE A PLAN TO GET IT. Base that plan on your strongest moves, and then ask yourself what kinds of grip, stance, position etc. you need to make them work and come out ready to impose those upon your opponent.

Very often in the sport of Jiu jitsu seems obvious what the problem you are confronted with as you grapple; but deeper analysis reveals that it was something quite different. Let's use the arm bar (juji gatame) as an example. On the surface juji gatame is all about your opponent's ELBOW, as ultimately your goal is to be able to apply breaking pressure to the elbow joint that forces my opponent to either submit or face the consequences. Once you begin studying juji gatame however, it becomes clear that central problem you are confronted with is that of HOW WILL YOU CONTROL YOUR OPPONENTS HEAD AND SHOULDERS WITH YOUR LEGS as you will never able to apply breaking pressure to the elbow until the head and shoulders are pinned by your legs. Once you change your focus from the elbow to the head the move becomes much more successful until you come to see the final step of juji gatame - breaking the elbow - as little more than an afterthought. Your initial battle is always that of your legs versus your opponent's head and shoulders. It is of the greatest importance that you take all your favorite moves and analyze them in this fashion. Constantly ask yourself what the primary problems for that move are - you will be surprised how often what are commonly thought of as the primary problems are secondary problems and the real issue are quite different from what many believe.

HE WHO CONTROLS THE HANDS CONTROLS THE BEGINNING OF EVERY EXCHANGE: In the vast majority of grappling encounters ENGAGEMENT WITH THE OPPONENT BEGINS WITH THE HANDS. As such, if we can dominate our opponent's hands as we first engage with them in a given scenario, we will have a significant advantage for the rest of the ensuing action. Make a habit of fighting to control your opponent's hands and you will soon it is much harder for opponents to control and attack you. This advance pertains to some scenarios more than others. For example, escaping a mounted pin is not dependent upon hand control and so it is much less important here; but other scenarios, such as defending and escaping rear mounts, are very much dependent upon good control of your opponent's hands. Identify the scenarios where hand control is crucial and experiment with different grips and strategies to dominate your opponent's hands - you will be impressed by

how often this strengthens your initial defense
and offense.

A RELAXED BODY MOVES BETTER AND MOVES LONGER THAN A TENSE ONE: Jiu Jitsu is a competitive combat sport - so it's only natural that you should physically tense up when the action begins. Be aware however that excessive physical tension is a potential pitfall that has sent many of us into early exhaustion and failure. Keeping a loose and relaxed demeanor whilst grappling in a competitive match is a difficult thing to do. Moreover, we can't be loose all the time. There are times when maximal tension may be needed to finish a move. In addition, we don't want to be so loose that you flop around ineffectively. Finding the right amount of tension vs relaxation at the appropriate times is a long-term study. Understand however, that it's an IMPORTANT study, as your ability to relax when you will be a BIG part of what determines your endurance levels in long tough matches - much more so than your cardiovascular fitness level. Start out by learning to relax yourself whenever you disengage with your opponent. Then start to expand upon this by learning to relax when caught in a pin or inferior position. Then try to get more relaxed even in the neutral positions so that you spend most of a match in a relatively relaxed demeanor. Soon you will notice your ability to move fluidly in response to your opponent's movements improves, along with the length of time you can engage with a tough opponent. Look how relaxed Nicky Ryan looks as he enters a training partners open guard - getting to that level of relaxation in sparring takes time, but the potential benefits make the effort worthwhile

The sport of Jiu jitsu is evenly divided between offensive and defensive skills. It's natural to want to focus more on the former as it is generally more fun and glamorous. Be aware however, that it will be your mastery of defense that will prove the more important when you come up against very good opponents who will be attacking you at least as much as you attack them (and in many cases - a lot more). While defense may not be as sexy as offense - those are the skills you will draw upon in a crises - and let me tell you - when you go against someone your own level or better - Jiu Jitsu is very much a sport of crisis management. Make sure you devote AT LEAST fifty percent of your training/development time to defensive skills. Those skills may not be as much fun to train but whatever unhappiness that training time may cause you is nothing compared with the unhappiness of losing a bout due to underdeveloped defensive skills. Balance your training time accordingly.

STOP MOVEMENT FIRST - break second: Ever tried to hit a moving target with a punch? You quickly learn it's a lot a harder than hitting a stationary one. So too in grappling. Breaking or strangling a moving opponent is usually significantly more difficult than one who has been immobilized. So, take your time to first focus on IMMOBILIZATION and only when that has been satisfactorily achieved, switch to the task of breaking/strangling. There is a reason why some submission holds have a higher success rate than others - its most due to the ability of that hold to immobilize an opponent. That's one of the main reasons why it is the most successful of all the arm locks in competition. So, when it's time to okay the submission game - divide your task in two. Focus first on restricting your opponent's movement. Only then go on to the subsequent task of finishing. You may not be able to do it every time, but when you can, you will be impressed by the results.

IN THE MAJORITY OF CASES it is not so much any one submission attack that determines the outcome but rather YOUR ABILITY TO MAINTAIN A POSITION THAT ALLOWS YOU TO MAKE MULTIPLE SUBMISSION ATTACKS THAT CREATE WITHERING PRESSURE THAT BREAKS AN OPPONENT DOWN UNTIL THE FINAL SUBMISSION ATTEMPT GETS THE BREAKTHROUGH. This is the meaning behind "position before submission." Each successive attack has a higher chance of breaking through as your opponent fatigues and must take greater and greater risks to make an escape. Remember always that the greatest submission hold of them all is PRESSURE OVER TIME and that the basis of pressure in Jiu Jitsu is position.

WHEN THE ARMS CAN'T GET THE BREAKTHROUGH YOU SEEK - LET YOUR LEGS DO THE WORK: A fundamental feature of the human body is the discrepancy between our upper body which is weak and tires quickly, and our lower body which is strong and possesses remarkable endurance. So often we grapple predominantly with the upper body because it feels more coordinated and responsive than our untutored lower bodies. When attacking the back, it's good to take advantage of the precise movement and dexterity of the arms to apply our strangles. However, if our opponent has strong defensive hand fighting skills we often get shut out. That's when it's time for you to bring in the power of the legs. The best method is that of utilizing the incredible power of the triangle - USHIRO SANKAKU. This will quickly overwhelm your opponent's hand defenses and often give you the victory.

Good Jiu Jitsu players are always very wary of keeping their elbows and knees close to their torso. This makes it very difficult to apply joint locks to them. If you could get those elbows and knees moving out and away from the torso - the submissions would come a lot easier. One of the very best ways to do this from bottom position is Kuzushi (off balancing). We humans are hard wired to prioritize balance - so when we lose balance we get distracted from all other concerns as we try to right ourselves. That's all the opportunity you need to enter your joint locks. When working from bottom position - ATTACK HIS BALANCE FIRST AND HIS LIMBS SECOND and watch your success rate increase.

WORKING FOR AN ANGLE: A foundational principle of Jiu Jitsu is to always seek some form of preliminary advantage prior to attacking. One of the best forms of advantage is ANGLE. If you can get away from being directly in front of opponents and instead get to the flanks, you will find a lot more success with many of your attacks. Constantly look to get your head offline and hips out to the side - often it will help to use an arm to grip inside your opponent's leg and manually pull yourself around to an angle. Now it will be difficult for an opponent to use his weight and top position to control you - Indeed, if he tries to use weight this may even make things worse for him. Don't settle for being held directly in front of opponents - work immediately for angle. Your opponent will have to react to this threat - if he doesn't you will have an immediate advantage - as he reacts you will find your attacking opportunities. Experiment tomorrow with making your first move every time from bottom closed guard just a simple shift to an angle and be prepared to work from there towards victory.

UNTYING A KNOT: Have you ever had the experience of trying to untie a big and complicated knot? Sometimes there can come a point where you just get so frustrated that you just pull aimlessly on the two ends of rope knowing that it will only serve to make the knot tighter. Many of the situations you will face in Jiu Jitsu have a similar nature. Sometimes it's so tempting just to yank and pull and push, even when the better part of us knows that it will have no effect. Learning to overcome our impulses and have the discipline to exercise the PROBLEM-SOLVING side of our mind rather than the impulsive emotional side is a big step towards maturity in Jiu Jitsu. Next time you feel that urge to just apply force without a plan, stop yourself ask yourself the two critical questions you must address in these situations. WHAT IS THE PROBLEM I AM CONFRONTED BY? And WHAT WOULD CONSTITUTE A SOLUTION TO IT. Remember - it's training - you can always stop and puzzle it out. Then the next time that

knot ties up your game you will have the
satisfaction of picking it apart and taking a
straight line to victory.

HAND CONTROL: The vast majority of moves in Jiu Jitsu require the use of the hands to form effective connection to an opponent so that the various moves can be performed. As primates, humans are hand-centric animals in all things - Jiu Jitsu included. As such, if we can control our opponent's hands, we can do a lot to shut down his offense. When you take on a dangerous gripper, make sure you pay attention to the possibility of shutting down his game by controlling his hands whenever possible. Just be sure that you do not do it in a way that makes you a negative player whose only concern is stopping the other fellow doing what he wants to do. Always take the action back in the positive direction of offense. So, once you establish hand control - go into your attacks rather than just aim to frustrate an opponent's offense at the hands. - I am sure you can see some offensive possibilities starting to emerge out of the initial hand fight.

ONE JIU JITSU - TWO PATHS: Two great combat athletes who took two very different paths with their Jiu Jitsu training work out next to each other. Keenan Cornelius works out next to Georges St-Pierre on a crowded mat in class today. One of the great features of Jiu Jitsu is the way the same techniques can be used in very different ways in very different arenas to get you to your own unique goals. Mr. Cornelius took his Jiu Jitsu training towards grappling, Mr. St-Pierre took it towards MMA - both became great champions in their respective domains. It fascinating to see such different athletes learning and performing the same moves but knowing each will have to find ways to apply them in very different contexts. Jiu Jitsu is a very malleable art that gives us a lot a choice in how we apply it. The foundations of the sport are broad enough that two entirely different careers can be lived while learning similarly next to each other just through adaption and the addition of other skills.

THE CURIOUS CASE OF HALF GUARD: Here's an odd thing - many of the most respected Jiu Jitsu authorities claim that getting to top half guard is one of the very best guard passing strategies in the sport and so advocate forcing your way to half guard as a superior passing strategy. Just as many respected Jiu Jitsu authorities claim that bottom half guard is one of the premier sweeping positions in the sport and so advocate actively getting to half guard whenever playing bottom position so that you can sweep an opponent. How can this be? How can the same position be seen as both the most desirable top position and at the same time the most desirable bottom position for the respective athletes? I am part of this seeming contradiction myself. I always encourage my students to actively work to get to half guard whenever they can and exploit its strengths as a passing position. Yet I also claim that bottom half guard is a great position to play for sweeps and submissions. How can you have it both ways? Much of the answer is bound up with THE CONTROL (or lack of) OF THE BOTTOM PLAYERS HEAD AND SHOULDERS. If the top player can pin the bottom players head and shoulders (usually through some variation of under hooks and cross faces) then yes, it's a superior passing position. If not, and the bottom player can move his head and shoulders as he pleases (usually by getting his own under hook to deny head and shoulder control to his opponent), then it becomes a very fine sweeping position for the bottom athlete. This fundamental element of control or denial of control of the bottom athlete's head and shoulders determines much of the action in half guard. All the other battles you will face in this position, distance control, Kuzushi/balance, grip etc. are most fought over either getting control of the bottom athletes head and shoulders or actively seeking to deny that control - depending on whether you are on top or bottom. See in this light you can see how one position can be both the path to heaven and hell depending upon the outcome of the crucial battle for head and shoulders.

GIVE A LITTLE TO GAIN A LOT: Sometimes when beginners get a good position on an opponent, they hold on so tight that the opponent cannot move at all. That's not wrong - it's a good thing to be able to immobilize an opponent. However, very often it is a good thing to allow your pinned opponent a little movement in a direction that can take you from a GOOD pin to a GREAT pin. Your opponent must move in order to escape. Oftentimes you can funnel their movement in directions that benefit you rather than him and make big positional gains as a result. Next time you get a good position, experiment with releasing pressure in beneficial ways. You may well find that you too, can gain a lot by giving a little

HALF GUARD AND CONNECTION: One of the distinguishing characteristics of a tight half guard with an under hook wrapped tight around your opponent's waist is the tremendous degree of CONNECTION it gives you to your opponent. Interestingly, this connection is easy even when your opponent is significantly taller and bigger than yourself. Contrast this with other guards - day closed guard - if you have short legs and your opponent has a thick midsection, it can be tough just to maintain a closed guard. In half guard you only must get your legs around one leg, rather than his waist or shoulders, so making that tight connection is easy, even when there is a big height or overall size difference. Moreover, the very nature of the connection places you DIRECTLY UNDER YOUR OPPONENT'S CENTER OF GRAVITY so even time you turn left or fight it have a big effect on an opponent's balance, making it a superb sweeping position. Because there is so much physical connection your body weight functions like an anchor upon your opponent's body and dramatically SLOWS THE PACE OF THE MATCH DOWN as long as you maintain the position. This can be a real advantage when matched against a younger, faster, athletically gifted opponent, so half guard perfect for older or slower athletes who do better when the pace is taken down a notch or two. So, if you are looking for a means of increasing your effectiveness from bottom position but feel that your mobility, age or body type may be a hindrance, investigate half Guard as a possible solution to your problems. Many fine athletes have built a career around this great position - perhaps you can be one of them

DISTANCE CONTROL AND HALF GUARD: One of the great problems associated with the use of half guard is that of DISTANCE CONTROL. Your opponent in top position will usually be looking to get right chest to chest contact and control your head and shoulders. If he can do so you will have almost no means of controlling the distance between yourself and your opponent for the simple reason that you will have no means of PUSHING WITH YOUR LEGS TO CREATE SPACE. Once an opponent gets to half guard chest to chest, your legs can only PULL. One way to combat this problem is the use of an initial knee shield using the knee of your top leg positioned at the hip or sternum. This gives you what you need to control distance - the ability to use a leg to push and create space. This can be used to halt your opponent's initial forward drive, and then to give you the space needed to come up with an under hook around your opponent's waist that will create an attacking half guard position where your opponent will not be able to establish control over your head and shoulders. Used well, that knee shield can give you the attacking half guard you seek rather than strong passing position on top that your opponent seeks. As a general rule I like to position my knee shield at the hip when working without the gi, and at the sternum when I can reinforce it with my collar grip with the gi. Play around with the knee shield as a means of initially controlling distance so you can get the half guard positioning YOU want rather than the one your OPPONENT wants!

When you look at an average Jiu Jitsu match around half of the time is spent in what appears to be a hopeless tangle of limbs is in crazy inverted and back to front orientations that seemingly have little to do with combat. Yet in less than a second any one of those bizarre positions can be converted into a position that can result in broken limbs or devastating strangles. Some people do a better job of converting those strangle entanglements into winning positions than others - why? Probably the most important reason is that THEY HAVE A CLEAR SENSE OF WHERE THEY WANT TO GET TO which they can call upon in even the most confusing upside down, rolling double inversion and NAVIGATE THEIR WAY TOA FINISHING HOLD OR PIN. Therefore you must develop a few favorite positions that become so hard wired in your consciousness that you can find your way to them from anywhere, anytime any place. Just as even the most confused and disoriented drunk somehow always finds his way home - so too a good Jiu Jitsu player will always find his way back to his favorite holds and pins and prevail among chaos. Keep experimenting until you find your natural favorite submission hold or pin that seems to fit you like a glove and practice until you can see a way to it from everywhere.

BATTLES WON AND BATTLES LOST: When working from half guard it's important to understand that there are two major battles being fought, often at the same time - a battle for upper body grip dominance and a battle for lower body leg connection, balance and distance. It is very important to understand - YOU CAN LOSE ONE OF THOSE BATTLES AND STILL BE EFFECTIVE - BUT YOU CAN'T LOSE BOTH. The safest way to do this is via the most fundamental move in Jiu Jitsu - the elbow escape - IF YOU CAN WIN THAT LOWER BODY BATTLE YOU CAN TURN THE WHOLE SITUATION AROUND AND TURN YOUR OPPONENTS UPPER BODY GRIPS INTO A LIABILITY. Learning to identify the two battles, the relationship between them and how to surrender one if the situation demands it and focus on the other is a big part of your development in the very important bottom half guard game.

THE FOUNDATIONS OF YOUR GAME AND LEARNING NEW SKILLS: The fastest learners of my approach to the game are invariably those who have a STRONGLY DEVELOPED FOUNDATION OF BJJ SKILL. So often students come to me and ask to learn advanced systems that I teach but lack overall competence in foundational skills and so struggle to learn the additional skills. Having a strong set of foundational skills makes the act of adding on new skills very easy on most cases. The body movement, conceptual understanding and sensitivity that comes with learning the sports foundations translate extremely well into the more exotic elements of the game at higher levels. So, keep working hard on your fundamentals - there's never too much practicing and refining the core movements and skills of the sport. Time spent this way will dramatically shorten the time taken to add on new skills later.

AIM HIGH: The single biggest obstacle to the learning and improving process is LOW EXPECTATIONS AND STANDARDS AMONG THOSE SEEKING IMPROVEMENT. A huge part of realizing your potential in Jiu Jitsu and indeed anything else in life, is your ability to form a culture of high standards and great expectations around yourself. Days where you exhibit a "that's good enough" mentality are days wasted. Always ask the better question - "is my performance of this technique good enough to win a world championship." Just that switch in mindset from "is this good enough to get by?" to "is this good enough to work on a world champion?" Will immediately drive you to better performance of that move. THE FIRST STEP TOWARDS HIGHER PERFORMANCE AGAINST OTHERS IS HIGHER STANDARDS AND EXPECTATIONS WITHIN YOURSELF. Make a habit of comparing yourself to ever greater standards and you will soon see improvement in your technique

USING YOUR HEAD: The phrase "using your head" usually means to use your intelligence to perform a task better - that's a wonderful ideal that you should use at every opportunity - but in this instance I'm talking about using your actual head (not brain) to perform tasks in grappling. Your head is an incredibly important means of PUSHING an opponent. When you use it is often freeing up your hands to perform other tasks. You must actively seek to use your head whenever possible to move and control an opponent. A very big part of this sport is the PUSH/PULL DYNAMIC that underlies much of the game. Most people only push and pull with their hands and feet - give yourself a fifth pushing limb by actively using your head and you will have a big advantage over your four limbed opponent's - now THAT'S Using your head!

CREATION AND DESTRUCTION OF SPACE: Most of Jiu Jitsu is fought on the ground - as much the major dynamic between the two athletes plays out in TOP and BOTTOM position. It is crucial to understand that the top and bottom athletes have diametrically opposes general goals. From the top players perspective, the whole game is to ELIMINATE SPACE between himself and his opponent. By getting past the legs and using gravity getting in close and tight is the best way to control movement and dominate the bottom player. From the bottom players perspective, the whole game is to CREATE AND MAINTAIN SPACE so that he can move under the body weight of the top player and launch effective attacks from bottom position. All attacks require MOVEMENT and movement is only possible from bottom position when there is space between you and the top player. This basic demand for the creation and destruction of space is the heart and soul of the ground grappling game. Learning to understand the nuances that underlie this classic battle between top and bottom player is a huge part of your development in Jiu Jitsu.

KNOW THYSELF: A big part of success both short term and long term comes from knowing your own game well. In the short term self-knowledge helps you win today because you know what you're good and where you have weaknesses - so that when you take on a tough opponent you play mostly with what you do well and avoid what you do poorly. In the long term, self-knowledge will direct your training regimen. By identifying your weaknesses, you can devote extra training time to them with the goal of making your current weaknesses into future strengths. So, whether for today or tomorrow - self-knowledge is a critical part of your success. We all look in the mirror once a day to check our physical appearance - how often do you look in your Jiu Jitsu mirror and take a hard look at yourself - do it more often and do it with more care and you will be better equip for the challenges of today and the future.

LEGS ARE LIKE SEX PARTNERS - two is always
better than one: Controlling one leg in ashi
garami is good, but your opponent will always
use his other leg to defend the one you have
trapped. That is why I always distinguish
between the primary leg (the one trapped inside
your ashi garami) and the secondary leg (your
opponent's other leg). Whenever possible you
want to control BOTH legs as this will severely
impact your opponent's ability to use one leg to
defend the other. In addition, it creates an
immediate SHACKLING effect where your
opponent feels as though his two ankles are
shackled together in a way that robs him of any
athletic ability. This makes the task of CONTROL
much easier - but it creates a problem for the act
of BREAKING, as now you cannot attack both
legs simultaneously, but rather you must release
the secondary to attack the primary. This gives
an opponent a window of opportunity to escape.
LEARNING TO CLOSE THAT WINDOW TO THE
GREATEST DEGREE POSSIBLE WHILST

ACKNOWLEDGING THAT IT CAN NEVER BE TOTALLY CLOSED is the heart and soul of high percentage leg locking and a subject for a lifetime of study and refinement.

TAKE A BREATHER: Probably one of the more commonly asked questions I get is - how can I increase my endurance during sparring? All kinds of people advocate all kinds of methods of improving endurance. In truth I see little carry over from increased cardiovascular training to mat endurance for athletes who are already close to their ideal weight. Obviously if you are well overweight some simple cardiovascular exercise that results in losing weight and improving fitness will be a big benefit. However, if you are already in good shape and still getting tired, chances are that the problem is more one of EFFICIENCY IN ENERGY EXPENDITURE than of a need for greater cardiovascular capacity. A simple insight that can have immediate beneficial effects on your endurance during sparring is LEARNING TO TAKE SMALL BREAKS IN THE ACTION as you spar. You don't need to go one hundred percent at all times. Good players follow a pattern of hard work - rest - hard work - rest. This allows them to perform a task, get closer to a goal and then recuperate so as to repeat this pattern until the final goal is achieved. Jiu Jitsu is a positional game and there are many positions that offer a chance to take a brief rest and get your breathing and heart rate under control. Learn to identify safe zones where you can take a short break without great risk as you climb the ladder of position to your goal.

PUTTING THINGS TOGETHER: Nothing gets the breakthrough better than COMBINED ATTACKS. Defending one submission is tough, defending a well applied combination of submissions is hell - that is why I always try to create thorough SYSTEMS around the highest percentage submission holds - so that as one attack gets foiled another can take its place. Best of all however, is when you can LINK ONE SUBMISSION SYSTEM WITH OTHERS. Now it becomes extremely difficult to stop an unfolding attack that is expressing combinations both WITHIN a system and BETWEEN systems.

GETTING UNDER AN OPPONENT'S CENTER OF
GRAVITY: A key skill is grappling is that of
LIFTING AN OPPONENT OFF THE MAT. This is
done for many reasons. In Jiu Jitsu but is mostly
done from bottom position to set up sweeps and
lower body submissions. Understand that you
will never be able to lift people bigger and
heavier than yourself until you master GETTING
UNDER THEIR CENTER OF GRAVITY. only when
you can under their center of gravity will you be
able to lift them easily off the mat and into the
move you seek to perform. In standing grappling
this usually entails SINKING YOUR HIPS UNDER
THEIRS WITH A LEVEL CHANGE. In ground
grappling bottom position, it usually entails
SCOOTING YOUR HIPS DEEP UNDER THEIR
HIPS. When you do this, you can lift even very
big opponents. When you don't, you will be
unable to lift even a lightweight. If you want to
make a name for yourself as a dangerous
attacker from bottom position, Practice scooting

under and lifting daily and soon you will be attacking with much greater effect!

CAPTURING THE HEAD: The human body is essentially a skull connected to a spine and everything hangs off that - so when you control the head you control everything else by default. As such, we must put a very high priority on capturing the head whenever we can. THE WHOLE POSITIONAL GAME OF JIU JITSU IS DESIGNED TO GET US PAST OUR OPPONENTS LOWER BODY UP TO THE MID BODY AND THEN PROGRESS UP UNTIL WE CAPTURE THE HEAD. Most of the time we capture the head with our arms, but you can do it in very impressive ways with your LEGS also - via the TRIANGLE (sankaku). Remember always the GOAL of the positional game - HEAD CONTROL. Whenever you have the opportunity to control the head - take it - and control of the rest of the body will be your reward.

CLOSING DISTANCE: The whole game in Jiu Jitsu or indeed, any grappling art, is to get close and come to grips with your opponent. The act of getting close enough to establish contact - CLOSING THE DISTANCE - is a skill like any other in Jiu Jitsu and must be practiced and developed. Unfortunately, most people just assume that the opponent will engage in grappling and move forward rather lackadaisically and complacently reach out to grab an opponent with about as much technique and tactics as they employ reaching for a milk shake. In a competitive match you will have to fight just to establish basic contact with a skilled opponent. You must have a method of closing distance and getting to advantageous grips. Understand this - ATHLETES WHO START WELL GENERALLY FINISH WELL. Don't just approach and grab - APPROACH WITH A PLAN TO SECURE EARLY ADVANTAGE THAT WILL FACILITATE GETTING TO EVEN BIGGER ADVANTAGES.

FIFTY PERCENT OF JIU JITSU IS DENYING YOUR OPPONENT THE SAME THINGS YOU AIM TO DO TO HIM. We all practice as much as possible the things we want to do to our opponent - but at least fifty percent of your time should be spent in those skills of denial - of STOPPING HIM FROM DOING WHAT HE WANTS. I love to see my students practice offense - but I make damn sure they never neglect their defense because we all have a natural tendency to under emphasize it. So, get out there and practice your skills of denial - the better your opponent's get - the more you will need them!

THE IDEAL OF JIU JITSU: My understanding of Jiu Jitsu never waivers from this - JIU JITSU IS THE ART AND SCIENCE OF CONTROL THAT LEADS TO SUBMISSION. The closer you stay true to this ideal, the more impressive your game will be. The further you stray from it; the less people will want to follow your example. The appeal of the greatest athletes in the sport is not just that they win, but HOW they win - and nothing catches our admiration more than the decisive and clean mature of victory by submission. The soul of wrestling is the pin, the soul of judo is the ippon throw - but the soul of Jiu Jitsu is submission. Every move, tactic, strategy and concept that I teach goes in that direction. I am proud to see my students express that ideal every time they go out on the stage. Encouraging my Jiu Jitsu ideal of control leading to submission isn't about rule sets - it's about mind set - make that ideal your goal and take the time to learn how to enact it and the soul of Jiu Jitsu will become part of your soul as an athlete.

the story of Nick Rodriguez: One of the most inspiring stories to come out of the ADCC World Championships is that of blue belt Nick Rodriguez. The young man from New Jersey was a former high school wrestler with an additional year of D3 college wrestling, took up Jiu Jitsu because he preferred the idea of a submission hold over a pin. Gordon Ryan brought him into the basement, and he would travel four hours a day to get to class and learn. In preparation for ADCC the great question was how to take a raw talent with very limited experience in the sport and get him ready for championships level opponents. Obviously, he was not going to win with pure Jiu Jitsu nor with pure wrestling. Step number one was to give him a cast iron defense to the biggest danger to a blue belt - submission holds. He soon became extremely difficult to control and finish. Next was the question of how he would win. In order to create a winner, you need to give them a skill that they do better than their rivals - but how do you make a blue belt better than Champion black belts? The answer was not wrestling but rather the fascinating INTERFACE between wrestling and Jiu Jitsu where there is a world of possibilities in scrambles for a well-prepared athlete to beat people he would ordinarily not be capable of beating. Mr. Rodriguez developed an amazing ability to scramble to the back in the grey zone between takedowns and ground and between bottom position and standing position. Once that was allied with our back-finishing system it created a monster who shocked the hell out of everyone in the gym - and then at ADCC - everyone in the grappling world! With a silver medal at the world championships in such a short time there is a valuable lesson here for all of us - start with a cast iron defense, then build an offense around your unique talents/skills that really works for you. Then go out there and ignore all the preconceptions people have about how long it takes to be competitive among the best - your skill level, not your years of training- determines the outcome

GRIP AND ATTACK: A common problem that many students run into once they start to develop favorite grips from which to launch their attacks is a natural tendency to get to a good grip and HESITATE, as though the grip will get better with time. GRIPS DON'T GET BETTER WITH TIME. Once you get your grip - ITS TIME TO GO! You don't have to set a speed record, but you don't want to procrastinate either. Grips almost always get worse with time as your opponent will invariably be trying to break free. So, build a habit of getting to your grip and moving seamlessly into the appropriate attacks from that grip. Train the grip and attack reflex and you will soon be experiencing more success with your favorite moves.

REFLECTIONS ON ADCC 2019 - the internationalization of grappling - Australia makes a statement: One of the great themes to emerge from the recent world championships in Anaheim California was the terrific performance of developing grappling countries. For most of its history the podiums of the world championships have been dominated by a single nation - Brazil. In time some great individuals emerged who won titles - mostly from the United States. This year two outstanding Australian athletes won medals and really impressed everyone with a very high submission rate over 75%! Craig Jones won silver in his weight category - the highest ever won by his nation. Lachlan Giles won bronze in the absolute division - a fantastic achievement for a 77kg grappler (I'm not sure but I think the only other person from 77kg to medal in absolute division was Marcelo Garcia - perhaps some of my readers can confirm/deny this). Craig Jones won every match via submission on his way to the final, showing great variation with three different submissions over three different parts of the body to reflect his rapidly growing versatility. Lachlan Giles hit three superb heel hook finishes on three MUCH bigger and stronger world champion opponents and brilliantly showcased the great ideal of Jiu Jitsu of lesser strength controlling and defeating greater strength. The work of these two young Australians is a clear statement - Jiu Jitsu belongs to the world. The future will see a growing internationalization that I think will be immensely helpful for its growth and development. If ADCC is to strengthen its role as the Olympics of grappling it must, as the Olympics does, reflect the work of the whole world. It was a wonderful thing to see Australia, a nation that has always punched far above its weight in sports representation, take the lead through these two brilliant athletes. Well done Craig and Lachlan and well done to the Australian grappling community who helped launch these two to the top of the grappling world. I am certain other developing grappling nations will follow this example and will soon see a truly international flavor to world championships in future years.

HANDICAP YOURSELF TO IMPROVE YOUR PERFORMANCE: When we think about performance improvement, we typically think of giving ourselves every possible advantage. However, one of the best ways to improve your overall performance levels is to deliberately handicap yourself in training and take away your advantages so that you can build up other, weaker aspects of your game that will be of great benefit in the future. Take the example of Nick Rodriguez. He is built like a titan and moves like a leopard. On any given day in the basement there may be only two or three people even close to his size and no one with his overall physicality. If wanted, he could simply overwhelm 95% of his training partners in sparring on physicality alone. That, however, would mean zero technical improvement over time - just the same workout and results every day until he got bored. Instead, he intelligently handicaps himself by starting in compromised positions and toned down the use of his explosive speed and strength so that he can practice the refinement of his technique and make technical progress. His intelligent approach to training paid off in the ADCC heavyweight division. In our training room he is always the biggest in the room - but in the heavyweight division his first opponent towered over him and outweighed him by around 30-40 pounds. His second opponent outweighed him by almost a hundred pounds. In his battle to the finals he had to defeat a Jiu Jitsu world champion and two former ADCC champions - all bigger or at least same size as he - an incredible task. If he had just run over all his smaller partners in the gym he never would have practiced the compromised positions you inevitably find yourself in against bigger more experienced opponents you will face in competition in your own weight category and probably would have lost; but his good training attitude gave him the competition skills he needed to get to the finals in one of the most impressive debut performances in ADCC history. Remember always - A GOOD HEAVYWEIGHT CAN GET A GREAT WORKOUT IN A ROOMFUL OF LIGHTWEIGHTS AND A GOOD BLACK BELT CAN GET A GREAT WORKOUT IN A ROOMFUL OF WHITE BELTS.

LIFE ISN'T FAIR - and neither should be your Jiu Jitsu: The whole point of Jiu Jitsu is to create an unfair advantage over your opponent - Jiu Jitsu is the art of making things as unfair in your favor as possible within the rules. The most well-known and important means of creating an unfair playing field is POSITION. If you get a dominant position on an opponent from where you can attack him whilst he cannot attack you, that is clearly going to make for a much easier match for you. Of all the various positions in sport Jiu Jitsu, I favor the back above all, and make it the centerpiece of our positional training. A big theme of my teaching is to GO BEYOND POSITION as a means of creating advantage and start bringing in other elements that create STILL GREATER ADVANTAGE until the fight becomes completely unfair in your favor. Gordon Ryan, a true master of creating unfair advantage from the back, goes far beyond positional advantage and ties up both of his opponent's defensive arms whilst leaving one of his arms free to strangle. Such is the effect of the arm traps he is using that one hand proved to be sufficient to finish a strangle in the final of the ADCC world championships against a very tough opponent. Look always to go beyond position and constantly seek to enlarge and improve your understanding of advantage in Jiu Jitsu. Understand always that the entire sport is built upon this philosophy and that the deeper your understanding of how to get mechanical and tactical advantage over an opponent the easier and more impressive your Jiu Jitsu will appear.

The moment you step up to a challenge on the mats, whether it be just another sparring round at the dojo or a big competition; it's natural to wonder about the abilities of your opponent. What are his best moves? What tactics will he employ? Will he be stronger or have better endurance than you? It good to pay some attention to your opponent, but don't go too far down that route, as in truth there will never be any certainty about those questions until the match is over. Put your primary emphasis upon knowing YOURSELF. Know what you are good and what you're not good at. Use that knowledge to develop a strong sense of identity - this is who I am, and these are my strong points - and seek always to push the match in those directions. You can't control who your opponent is or what his skills are - but you can definitely control who you are and what your skills will be. Any wishy-washy thoughts of "what will I do out there?" Must be replaced with a strong sense of who you are technically and stylistically and the will to show that to the opponent. Knowledge of WHAT YOU ARE GOOD AT and a sense of WHAT YOU STAND FOR in Jiu Jitsu will give you the clarity of purpose you will need to rise to whatever occasion you find yourself in.

PEOPLE TREAT YOU DIFFERENTLY WHEN YOU ARE DANGEROUS: A big theme in my coaching is that of PRECISION IN BREAKING MECHANICS. I insist to all my students that they study deeply the dark arts of breaking limbs and strangulation. Remember always that it is the submission holds of Jiu Jitsu that make it dangerous. When you have powerful breaking mechanics and you can snap limbs like matchsticks your opponent's treat you very differently from a strictly positional player. They start overreacting to threats and feints, they are reluctant to engage with you, they must settle for a tactical game of score and run rather than really engage with you. Learning to master the precise details is not fun - you must have it done to you to learn how to do it to others. You also must be very responsible with it as you can't afford to hurt training partners. But once you gain it, opponents will treat you with a respect that few are shown. Take time with a friend working on those all-important mechanics. Experiment with how changes in your opponent's position and body type require you to adapt the lock for maximum effect. There is a reason why all my senior students are feared for their breaking power. With training and experimentation, you can be too.

YOU'RE NEVER GOING TO FEEL GOOD ABOUT YOUR TRAINING SESSIONS - you're never going to feel one hundred percent going into a match: We all have a dream that one day our Jiu Jitsu will feel unstoppable and that the efforts of training will be rewarded with constant progress to a point where you win every match without effort and that our bodies will strengthen with the training to the point we feel physically perfect. This is a pipe dream. Your body will always have issues and pains and in most cases, you will have to face up to your challenges in a less than optimal physical state with nagging injuries and constant fatigue. In addition, understand that all your training partners are progressing at roughly the same rate as you and thus you will never have effortless victories in the gym. Every session will be a slog against the pains and fatigue inside your own body and the training partners who grow alongside you and remain a severe test every single session. This photo of Gordon Ryan was taken one week before his dominant double gold performance at ADCC. It shows clearly the strain of a standard daily training session (one of three per day). If you saw how effortless many of his matches looked at the world championships, you might think the training sessions were even more so - this picture tells a different story. ITS NEVER GOING TO BE AN EASY RIDE FOR YOU - don't think in those terms. The only measure of worth is this - ARE YOU SLIGHTLY BETTER AT THE SKILLS YOU ARE WORKING ON WHEN YOU WENT TO SLEEP THAN WHEN YOU WOKE. No matter how tired and beat up you might feel after your workouts, THAT'S a realistic and worthwhile goal for every session.

WHEN THE PRESSURE IS ON - It's good to have some weapons you truly believe in: Humans tend to be naturally risk averse. We generally tend to fear the risk of loss more than we cherish the prospect of gain. This tendency tends to become even stronger in high pressure situations. In Jiu Jitsu this will often result in athletes restricting themselves to only their most trusted moves when they are on the big stage. It is crucial for your development therefore, that you have a select arsenal of moves in which you have total trust. These are the guns that you will be willing to fire when the heat is on - all those other moves that you like and enjoy when you are rolling with your friends in the gym won't do you any good now. At ADCC 2019 Garry Tonon fought for the bronze medal and took on the very talented and physically powerful Dante Leon, who had impressed everyone by defeating Jiu Jitsu legend Lucas Lepri in an earlier round. When it came time to attack, Mr. Tonon went back to one of

the most recognizable of the squad arsenal -
outside heel hook from outside ashi garami - a
move he has drilled and performed many
thousands of times. Despite the tense nature of
the match his confidence in the move, derived
from so much practice and experience in its use
and application, meant that there was not a
second of hesitation and once again it was
outside ashi garami heel hook for the win! You
too, must develop a small but very strong subset
of moves that are your most trusted weapons
upon which you can call when the pressure is on
you to perform. Your selection is an expression
of your body and your personality so this is a
deeply personal part of your development and
no one else can tell what your selection will be -
but select them over time you must, for when
you are too nervous to try your other moves -
these guns will still fire.

something of value that is true, but which only a
few people KNOW or ACKNOWLEDGE is true.
For example, I knew many years ago that leg
locks could be improved from their basic format
and made into a system just as effective as
traditional Jiu Jitsu upper body submission and
position orthodoxy. When I taught that to the
squad it gave them a significant advantage that
enabled them to effectively match up against
athletes with far more overall experience than
them and win. If everyone acknowledges the
truth of a true idea, then it's difficult to use it to
advantage - but if an important idea is true AND
YOU ARE THE ONLY ONE WHO BELIEVES IT TO
BE THE CASE - THEN YOU CAN EASILY USE IT
TO YOUR ADVANTAGE. A good example of this is
one of my favorite moves - which I believe has
always been massively undervalued in Jiu Jitsu.
This is the rear triangle (ushiro sankaku). It is a
truly devastating weapon, far more controlling

than the more popular arm bars and strangles normally used in this position. From it you can apply a crushingly powerful strangle and many joint locks. It offers far more control than its alternatives and truly enables a smaller person to defeat a bigger person. All my senior students are masters of it - you should be too! Make a serious study of ushiro sankaku and take advantage of other people's failure to see the value of this gold mine of submissions!

PATHWAYS TO THE BACK: You all know how much emphasis I put on getting to the back. In a pure grappling match without strikes I value the back mount far more than the front mount EVEN THOUGH THEY SCORE THE SAME AMOUNT OF POINTS. As such, a big part of our coaching program is spent of developing pathways to the back from anywhere. All my students excel in this, particularly the Ryan brothers. An interesting point about this notion of constantly seeking the back is that whilst it is mostly a physical skill, there is also a mental component insofar as you first must identify the OPPORTUNITY. You must train your eyes to see the opportunity before you pull out the move to realize that opportunity. The world is full of Jiu Jitsu students who know many moves to take the back, but who overlook myriad opportunities in live sparring and so never get to use those moves when it counts. I often preach to my students IF YOU CAN SEE THE BACK, YOU CAN TAKE THE BACK. While this is an oversimplification and there is more to the story than this, it does a good job of getting students to MENTALLY IDENTIFY OPPORTUNITIES to take the back - the single most important first step towards back mastery. Next time you are sparring keep those eyes of yours looking for the back and I promise you will find yourself more often on your opponent's back!

FIGHTING SMALLER PEOPLE: One of the great themes of Jiu Jitsu is that of constantly developing your ability to OVERCOME GREATER STRENGTH WITH LESSER STRENGTH. As such much is written and talked about how to beat bigger opponents. In contrast, little is spoken about how to beat smaller opponents. The feeling is that bigger people ought to be able to beat smaller people just in virtue of being bigger. However, I'm sure you have all had the unpleasant experience of going up against a tricky smaller fighter and really struggling with the task. In the recent ADCC World championships open weight division exactly this scenario played out - 77kg division entrant Lachlan Giles had been beaten in his first match in his own weight division and went into the open weight as a heavy underdog as one of the smallest entrants. He used the classic weapons of the smaller athlete - inversion, inside positioning and off balancing to successfully attack three much larger heavyweights and win by submission - one of the outstanding performances of the event. Underestimating the smaller athlete resulted in three heavyweight world champions getting soundly defeated (lack of knowledge of the leg lock game was also an obvious factor). It was a valuable lesson to the Jiu Jitsu World - we can't ignore the question of how to take on smaller opponents. Gordon Ryan took on Mr. Giles during his heavyweight blitz. We decided that the two best options would either finish him with counter leg locking as he appeared vulnerable to some strong counter opportunities and Mr. Ryan has an extremely strong leg lock and counter leg lock game that the other heavyweights clearly lacked; or play a game based on the two biggest problems bigger athletes can create for smaller athletes - nullify the effects of the legs and inversion by stepping over a knee and getting chest to chest to maximize weight advantage and minimize movement from underneath, then get behind where height advantage creates tremendous control and submission opportunities through arm traps with body triangles. The second option arose first and here you see the result - but make sure you have a plan for ALL opponents big AND small.

Probably the single most iconic Jiu Jitsu position and the one that we all started with is closed guard. While mount and rear mount are the most dominant positions, there is nothing surprising about their dominance. If a total grappling neophyte saw them, he would intuit very easily that they are superior positions conferring great advantage to the player in the attacking position. But if that same neophyte saw a closed guard and you tried to tell him that the bottom closed guard player had a tactical advantage over the top player - he may well call you a fool - after all, he is in bottom position in a situation that looks more appropriate for the bedroom than winning fights. Yet the bottom player assuredly does have a tactical advantage in a grappling situation from bottom closed guard. As long as the guard is closed, the top player cannot engage in any serious positional or submission attacks. All he has are a few very low percentage options that are very likely to be strongly countered by a good bottom player. He cannot initiate any serious positional or submission offense until he first opens the guard. The bottom athlete on the other hand, can immediately begin attacking from closed guard with some of the best submission and positional attacks in the sport. There is a powerful asymmetry here between the top players inability to do much until he first opens the closed guard versus the bottom players ability to attack very strongly from the same situation. Learning to gain faith in this tactical advantage is a BIG part of your early development in bottom game Jiu Jitsu. In time you can make yourself a nightmare to anyone trapped inside your closed guard - to the point where opponents fear it almost as much as your mount or rear mount. That journey begins with understanding and trusting in the tactical asymmetry in attacking opportunity between top and bottom player in closed guard. It may not be obvious to the neophyte - but one day your ability to exploit this will identify you as an expert!

A MAN OUT OF BALANCE IS EASY TO ATTACK:
Attacking and scoring in Jiu Jitsu on someone your own level is never easy. Understand this: THE DEGREE OF DIFFICULTY ASSOCIATED WITH ATTACKING A SKILLED OPPONENT IS DIRECTLY PROPORTIONAL TO THE STRENGTH OF HIS POSTURE AND BASE. If you can break his posture and base by upsetting his balance - the attacks come MUCH easier. Whenever you play bottom position, always seek to get gravity working in your favor by constantly attacking your opponent's base of support. My favorite way of doing so is foot techniques - in particular foot sweeps (ashi waza). Well applied foot sweeps from bottom position can make your opponent miserable and make it very difficult for him to settle down into strong passing positions and at the same time, greatly facilitate your favorite attacks. Ideally you want to create a situation where he finds it very difficult to stand in front of you and is reduced to stumbling around like a drunk on roller skates

while you can dart into your favorite moves. After the stumble there will be a momentary opportunity to go easily into attack and score. Take it and win!!

MANY PEOPLE GO OUT ON THE STAGE THINKING THEY ARE GOING TO WIN - only a few go out KNOWING they are going to win. Your job is to train in such a manner that over time you become more like the latter and less like the former. Your first steps involve developing a clear understanding of all the means by which you could possibly lose a match and making it impossible for an opponent to make them happen. Once you know an opponent has no means of scoring on you - the act of winning becomes a lot easier.

TIME: Of all the critical factors that go into success in Jiu Jitsu the one that gets talked about the least and yet which probably ought to be talked about the most is the effect of time. There are three main ways in which time plays a decisive role in outcomes. The first is SPEED OF DECISION-MAKING RELATIVE TO YOUR OPPONENT. Your job is to make better and faster decisions than the other fellow. If you can do this consistently you will almost always win. You want to solve the problems he creates for you faster than he can solve the problems you create for him. The second is the time lag between MAKING A DECISION AND ACTING UPON IT. We all constantly second guess and procrastinate. You don't have to be the fastest man out there in a physical sense, but the faster you can go from DECISION to ACTION the better you will do. The world is full of people who know what they ought to do but delay pulling the trigger - that's why failure is so prevalent. The third way in which time plays a role is more pertinent to competition. HOW MUCH TIME IS LEFT IN THE MATCH? This will heavily influence your choice of technique and tactics. Make sure you have techniques that are divided up by how much time it takes to execute them and there is considerable variation in this regard. This will determine our selection of technique - in this case, lots of time so a time consuming but very high percentage moves such as a rear strangle is appropriate - and in this case, an excellent path to victory.

CLOSED GUARD - ANGLE IS EVERYTHING: The closed guard is one of the most representative of classic Jiu Jitsu among of all the major positions. Even if you don't favor it yourself, you can be assured that other people will often use it on you - so the more that you know about it the better - no exceptions. One of the main routes to success from bottom closed guard is ANGLE. It is difficult to perform any kind of successful offense without first getting misaligned with your opponent. You must make a habit of constantly misaligning yourself if you are to become a threat from bottom. Your opponent will seek to counter by re-aligning himself to you. In that action/reaction exchange of alignment vs misalignment if the game of closed guard. Your hips are the basis of the position and you want yours out an angle. This might be something as a small shift to one side that creates enough space to enter a triangle, or it could be a turn far beyond ninety degrees that enables you to spin and rise into an arm bar. In almost every case, some form of misalignment to an angle will be required to generate attacks. Remember always that there is a world difference between being on the back vs being FLAT on your back. It's tough to be effective when you are flat on your back in bottom position - but the simple act of constantly shifting your hips from side to side and gaining angles big and small will help greatly to improve your offensive potential from this great position.

FAILURE AND SUCCESS: A moments reflect reveals that THE VAST MAJORITY OF SUBMISSION ATTEMPTS WE MAKE IN THE COURSE OF OUR JIU JITSU WILL END IN FAILURE. For every time we successfully apply a submission hold, we typically fail more than ten times. It's easy to get discouraged. It can even happen in the midst of a match. You have a favorite move - you try it several times and fail each time. It's easy to say to yourself that this opponent is impervious to this form of attack and stop trying and move on. Understand that in most cases it is only the imperfections in your application of the move that resulted in that failure - not the move itself or your opponent's defenses. When you experience failure, don't immediately assume this opponent can't be beaten by this method. Instead, try to asses on the spot how good your attempt was and what deficiencies lead to the initial failure - so that when you attempt it again you are doing a better job. If we just repeat the first failed attempt, you can only expect a second failure. But if you quickly assess what made the initial attempt fail and change those elements on the second or third attempt - you have a great chance of getting the breakthrough even after several initial failures. Never tell yourself "this isn't working." Rather, ask yourself, "why didn't that last attempt work?" The former leads to defeatism, the latter to confidence and success.

THE MOST READILY AVAILABLE MOVE IN THE SPORT - FRONT HEADLOCK: Jiu Jitsu is a sport that prioritizes getting close to your opponent and getting to grips with him. As such there is a lot of aggressive forward movement towards an opponent and a lot of level changing down to get under your opponent's defensive arms and get a hold of him. This results in MANY opportunities to take a front headlock upon your opponent. In fact, I would venture to say that front headlock is probably the single most available move/hold in Jiu Jitsu. It offers immediate control of the head - the most valuable part of the body to control when you want to restrain a powerful foe. It leads immediately into some of the best submissions in the sport - all guillotine variations and many kata gatame variations such as Darce and Anaconda strangles. In addition, it leads naturally to the back - king of all attacking positions - along with many fine takedown opportunities. It is equally effective in both standing and ground grappling and it is equally effective as a defensive move and an offensive move. If you get into a serious grappling match with a good opponent for more than two minutes, I GUARANTEE at some point there will be an opportunity for a front headlock - it's almost impossible to engage in grappling without either conceding the opportunity or being presented with the opportunity. As such you have two duties towards the front headlock. First, you should invest the time into developing a strong front headlock of your own. Second, you should have some strong and trusted defenses to the move given the very high likelihood you will have to fight out of it pretty much every time you grapple. Craig Jones took the time this year to vastly improve his front headlock skills in the blue basement and it showed at the ADCC World Championships where he used it extremely well en route to a silver medal with a seventy five percent submission rate! You must work this position and come to understand it's incredible potential and value.

PUT SOME VENOM IN IT! Most of my job is getting performance increases in Jiu Jitsu athletes. By far the biggest part of that job is increasing skill levels and improving tactics. As such I put a high value on technical nuance and sophistication among the people I teach. This is reflected in class where praise is usually directed to the pupils making the gains in technical performance. Most of our sparring tends to be very controlled with a big emphasis on excellence of execution. Nonetheless when it's time to shine on the big stage one must go beyond technique and start talking about INTENTION. When you must derive maximum performance from a given move there is an ineffable element that comes from the intensity of intention that you bring into the move. There is a BIG difference between sparring with someone who is calmly going through the mechanics of a heel hook versus someone who comes at you with the real intention of breaking your leg. Mental intention creates a unity of purpose in your body that creates a more powerful physical action. You don't want to train all the time with this, since training is more about physical refinement, but it's nice to add it into the mix periodically to see how much more venom you can add to the moves you practice every day. Technical perfection plus hard intention creates an unstoppable and intimidating move.

DENIAL: All the techniques of Jiu Jitsu are divided into two camps. First there are the positive offensive movements which involve our attempts to impose our moves upon an opponent. Second, there are the negative defensive movements where we try to deny our opponents ability to impose his moves upon us. Excellence in Jiu Jitsu is about mastery of BOTH types of technique. A big part of our opponent's ability to impose his moves upon us is bound up with his ability to get effective HANDLES upon us. If he can do so, then he can move us around, disturb our balance, work to a dominant grip etc. etc. Whenever you are in defensive situations then, BEGIN BY DENYING EFFECTIVE HANDLES ON YOUR BODY TO YOUR OPPONENT. There are certain points of the human body that give excellent handles to a skilled opponent - YOU MUST PROTECT THESE IMMEDIATELY WHEN PUT IN A COMPROMISED POSITION. learn to use your hands and elbows to cover up these handles early and you will soon find that subsequent defensive moves are MUCH easier than usual. The more you deny the main handles of the body to your opponent and the earlier you do it - the more effective your defensive game will be!

LACING YOUR OPPONENT'S LEGS: A very distinctive part of our leg lock system is preference for using the principle of DOUBLE TROUBLE whenever possible. Double trouble is the general principle that whenever you go to attack one leg, whether it be with a leg lock, a takedown or a sweep, ninety percent of the resistance comes from the OTHER leg. One of my favorite manifestations of this principle and one which all my students excel at - is a leg lace from cross ashi garami that binds and opponents two legs together and offers a tremendous degrees of control that can be used to hold, sweep and break an opponent who is considerably bigger, stronger and more athletic than you. Understand that almost all expressions of human athleticism require the unified work of both legs. When you shackle a man's legs together you rob him of all athleticism immediately - and a leg lace from cross ashi garami does exactly that. Look to utilize double trouble whenever you can - not just in leg kicking but across the board. You will be impressed how adherence to this principle can lower your workload whilst increasing your success rate.

Probably the most common question I am asked is - how do I defeat people bigger and stronger than myself. Here is my general advice. When matches against bigger people MAINTAIN INSIDE POSITION UNDERNEATH THEM AND CARRYING THEIR WEIGHT. IN OFFENSIVE SITUATIONS, FAVOR LEG ATTACKS AND MORE THAN ANYTHING ELSE - GET BEHIND THEM. Inside position is the key to managing greater body weight from underneath. The legs are the hardest thing for heavyweights to hide from a smaller and more agile player and once locked, a heel hook will break anyone regardless of size. Also, the bigger the foot, the longer the breaking lever and the less chance of slippage. And the back - I don't care how big and strong they are - they can't push or pull someone who is behind them - so get there soon and stay there to beat the big men! Nick Rodriguez is the biggest and strongest athlete in the blue basement by a landslide, but in ADCC World Championships he was rather small compared to some of his opponents. He took on the massively powerful two-time ADCC Champion Orlando Sanchez in his second match - gameplan? GET BEHIND HIM! He did exactly that and got the win! So, remember the basic strategy when fighting bigger, heavier and stronger people. Inside position when underneath, focus submissions on the legs and position on the back!

INSIDE POSITION: Jiu Jitsu is a game of control - my ideal is that it be a game of control that leads to submission - nonetheless it all begins with control. The most talked about means of control is POSITION. When people talk of position in Jiu Jitsu, they typically are referring to TACTICAL position i.e. how the two athletes are positioned relative to each other as defined by the scoring system of the sport - side position, mount position, rear mount position etc. But there is an entire different class of position that is just as important for control purposes - LIMB POSITION - i.e. how are my limbs positioned relative to my opponents limbs? The fundamental choice here is between OUTSIDE position (my limbs outside his limbs) and INSIDE position (my limbs positioned inside. Each has their good and bad points. When working from underneath a heavier opponent I generally recommend an emphasis on inside positioning. This makes it very difficult for an opponent to pin you by wedging his limbs around your torso and reinforcing those wedges with body weight for the simple reason that you are inside any wedge he can create. This enables you to create effective movement underneath an opponent's body weight - the basis of being effective from bottom position. Don't fear your opponent's weight - fear his ability to create immobilizing wedges around you - and inside control is a powerful antidote to this danger that has the added benefit of facilitating your own attacks.

THE REMARKABLE POWERS OF THE CROSS-LAPEL GRIP: There are no universal panaceas for the myriad problems and scenarios of Jiu Jitsu - we must be adaptable and look for individual solutions to every problem. Nonetheless there are some moves and concepts etc. that have incredibly wide applications and come as close to a panacea as we can get in this sport. One of them is the cross-lapel grip. This is probably the single most effective and versatile grip we can employ from guard position and many top pin scenarios as well. It is a grip that gives excellent and immediate control of your opponent's HEAD, arguably the most important part of the body to control. In addition, it creates an immediate danger of STRANGULATION to harass, intimidate and even finish an opponent. It gives a bottom guard player good distance control for both offense and defense. Perhaps most important it enables a bottom player to constantly BREAK AN OPPONENTS POSTURE and thus create strong action/reaction attacks as an opponent tries to resist and recover. Experiment with different ways of holding the grip based upon what end you want to achieve. Learn to switch hands and grip and re-grip side to side to lead actively into attacks rather than just holding on with a death grip without purpose. Create a sense of push/pull and action/reaction - this is the element that makes Jiu Jitsu interesting and artful rather than a slogging match. There is a reason why so many great athletes made this simple yet devastating grip the basis of their attacking grip game - make it part of yours too!!

YOU AREN'T GOING TO BE THE HAMMER EVERY TIME -
spend some practicing to be the nail: Jiu Jitsu is a
sport with two main elements - OFFENSE and
DEFENSE. Only by practicing BOTH will you
reach your potential in the sport. Of course
practicing offense is a lot more fun, but the fun
ends abruptly when you run into a tough
opponent who puts you in a defensive situation
and you realize you haven't trained for this at all
and you don't have the skills to hold him off. Set
time every session to practice the crucial skill of
defense. This sport is full of can crushers who
look amazing going against easy opponents but
who fold badly against studs. Only by regularly
training the less pleasant aspects of the sport do
you get the rare and wonderful ability to survive
a bad situation against a talented opponent and
fight back to victory.

There are many highways to an opponent's back - all of them are important - but the simplest and most direct and the one you need to master first - is to get outside your opponent's elbows. This can be done from standing, from top and from bottom. It can be done in many ways - arm drags, elbow posts, kata gatame etc. Make it a habit to constantly fight to get outside your opponent's elbows and you will always find yourself in an advantageous angle that will give you access to the back. As an added bonus, if the opponent defends his back by squaring up to you, he will make himself vulnerable to many submissions performed from frontal positioning or attacks on the other side of his body - all because of that initial threat you created by clearing his elbow. The elbow will always be the clearest and simplest demarcation line between frontal and back positions. Remember always that the back is the single best attacking position in all of grappling - learn to navigate your way there from everywhere and by every means - but understand that beating the elbow will be the most direct path you can take.

Most if the Jiu Jitsu is a battle against the clock. We must make decisions and perform moves in less time than our opponent if we are to put him under the kind of decision/action pressure that breaks people and lets us finish decisively. Strangling from the back is a different sort of affair. Unless there is limited time left in the match, you will generally get better results focusing on maintaining chest to back position and making sure you are securely hooked into both sides of his body first and only when these are preconditions met, switching focus towards the strangle. Understand that often position and control are partially lost as you attempt a strangle. Should this happen, STOP THE STRANGLE ATTEMPT AND RE-ESTABLISH CHEST TO BACK CONTACT AND CONTROL OF BOTH SIDES OF THE OPPONENTS BODY. Quite often there will be an extended period where you must fight for position and control on multiple occasions until finally you get the strangle opportunity. This is normal - TAKE YOUR TIME. Nothing is more heart breaking that getting all the way to the back and losing the position due to over zealousness. Craig Jones shows admirable poise and calm as he positions himself for a strangle. He is in no rush to strangle - there is no reason why he should be - WHEN YOU ARE IN A WINNING POSITION - LET THE POSITION DO THE WINNING FOR YOU. Let your position be the focus and you strangle merely an afterthought.

EVERY ATTACK FROM GUARD POSITION SHOULD BEGIN AS AN ATTACK UPON YOUR OPPONENT'S POSTURE AND BALANCE: To be effective from top position your opponent must work from a strong efficient posture and must be in balance. Your goal always is to take these two essential prerequisites away from him as soon and as often as possible. EVERY ATTACK YOU CAN MAKE FROM BOTTOM POSITION IS SIGNIFICANTLY EASIER WHEN YOUR OPPONENTS BALANCE AND POSTURE ARE BROKEN. You can break an opponent's balance forwards and backwards and side to side. Develop the skill of kuzushi (off balancing/posture destruction) and make it the basis of your guard game. Practice and refine the skill of knocking your opponent's hands, knees and hips down to the floor. As he tries to recover balance and stance your attacks will break through easily during that momentary distraction.

MAXIMIZING CONNECTION: Grappling is the business of controlling the movement of a resisting human being who is actively trying to control you as you try to control him. The means of control is PHYSICAL CONNECTION TO AN OPPONENT. Understand that connection comes in DEGREES. You can be more or less connected to an opponent. The more connection - the more control. As such, when it's time to control a limb to set up a submission, the onus is on you to make sure you maximize the contact and connection between his limb and your body. This will prevent the slippage and space that defeats so many submission attempts. You want focus upon getting the highest possible percentage of the surface area of his limb in contact with you and then to solidify that contact by setting wedges around that limb and using your hands and feet to set those wedges in place. Note how in this photo my hands work at the joints and my head provides supplemental wedging while my feet lock into the opponents legs - maximizing contact and locking it all in place to form a sound connection that will endure long enough even against strong resistance to get the job done.

A MASTER OF POSITION must perfect chest to chest and chest to back pins, but a master of SUBMISSION must go behind this and actively seek LIMB ISOLATION as the basis of his craft: The basis of offense in traditional Jiu Jitsu is position. Typically, this is understood in terms of getting past your opponent's legs and pinning him down either chest to chest or chest to back. However, the ability to submit an opponent requires you to go further and isolate a limb - to draw a limb away from the torso and away from the other limb. Only then can you break an opponent. Ultimately this will require you to develop subtle methods of wedging around a limb and trapping it in place long enough to apply the various submission holds of Jiu Jitsu - but your first step is MINDSET. Don't be satisfied with simply getting the chest to chest or chest to back positions. Train yourself to always think of going the extra step of LIMB ISOLATION after you get to a pin. Initially you will have some frustration here, as the act of isolating a limb often requires movement that can lessen control momentarily and result in an opponent escaping when performed poorly. However, only by persisting and developing this crucial skill will you make the jump from being a pinner to a finisher - the highest ideal of the sport. Look how Gordon Ryan uses an under hook to wedge an opponent's arm in place and move his elbow away from form his torso to isolate and weaken the arm. He has moved beyond the safety of chest to chest into the world of isolating wedges that lead to the possibility of submission - this is why his finishing percentages are so high. With patience and practice - so too can yours.

LET THE OTHER GUY FEEL THE STRESS: A common problem I observe is that of athletes doing a good job getting to a dominant position and then trying too hard too quickly to get a submission and losing control of the position they worked so hard to attain. Unless there is limited time left on the clock, relax, the other fellow should be the one in panic mode - not you. Use the superior position to recompose yourself, recharge your lungs if necessary and formulate a plan to finish. If at any point you feel the danger of escape - PROTECT THE POSITION FIRST AND WORRY ABOUT THE SUBMISSION SECOND - you can always come back to that later. Using this simple pattern of exertion to gain a position followed by active rest and recomposing in that position to gather resources into a final push for submission allowed him to secure the stranglehold soon after this photo was taken.

BREAK THEM DOWN TO A HIP: One of the distinguishing characteristics of the revolution in leg locking that the squad brought in was the heavy emphasis on leg locking from bottom position. In the old days the vast majority of leg lock entries were from top position. Indeed, leg locking was largely seen as an alternative to guard passing. This created a lot of naive criticisms of leg locking that seem almost quaint nowadays. Students were told that leg locks were a bad idea because if it didn't work you would lose top position. Well - what if we entered from bottom position? Then there was no danger of positional loss - so that's where I put my emphasis. There are MANY great entries from bottom position into an opponent's legs - but be sure to realize that though your ENTRIES into the legs will be on a standing or kneeling opponent in your guard - be sure to knock your opponent's down to their hips/buttocks (or at the very least one knee) before you start working for your FINISHES. It is quite difficult and risky to try finishing as a skilled opponent stands over you. Much safer to off balance him down to a hip first and THEN start working for the finish. Remember always that the magic of ashi garami is that it has a dual nature - IT IS JUST AS GOOD FOR OFF BALANCING/SWEEPING AS IT IS FOR BREAKING PURPOSES. Use BOTH aspects of ashi garami from bottom position and your success rate from under tough opponents will start climbing in the directions you want!

PROTECT YOUR POSITION FIRST BUT KEEP YOUR
EYES OPEN FOR THE POSSIBILITY OF SUBMISSION AT
ALL TIMES: We humans are prone to tunnel
vision, particularly in stressful situations. Very
often we get to a good position and remember
our mantra to protect the position first and
everything else second and as a result, we blind
ourselves to great opportunities to enter a
submission hold that were there right in front of
us. Look at this photo of Gordon Ryan - master of
back attacks - attacking from his favorite
position. His body has contoured perfectly to his
opponents, forming a tight connection and his
head and hip position will enable him to easily
follow an opponent's movement. However,
notice that his eyes are focused entirely on the
neck - the target of submission. So though his
body is set upon maintaining position, his mind
is set upon submission - indeed, he has unlocked
his hands already to take advantage of the open
neck he is looking so intently at and a few
seconds later he will be locking in a powerful

strangle. Condition yourself to think the same way. Let your body protect the position, but keep your mind focused like a laser on the next step - submission!

DON'T WORRY ABOUT THE SPEED WITH WHICH YOU MOVE - concern yourself with the distance you must cover: Very often I am asked by students if they are too slow to be effective in Jiu Jitsu. Certainly, it's an impressive thing to see an athlete with blazing speed in the mats. In truth however, most of the finest players in the sport work at a rather slow pace for most of the match and many more never really use speed at all in their game. Clearly then speed is not essential to success, though it can be useful at times. Understand that because Jiu Jitsu is predominately a ground sport, speed will always be limited. A much more important consideration than top speed is the DISTANCE YOU HAVE TO COVER TO GET TO YOUR OBJECTIVES. If I have a speedy opponent who moves twice as fast as I do, but through inefficient positioning and course setting, always must move twice as far to get to his objectives we will be working at effectively the same mat speed. Indeed, I will be able to sustain that mat speed longer since I am doing less work and may end up being faster as fatigue becomes a factor. The first step to becoming faster on the mats is to become more efficient at covering distance to get to an objective. THE MORE DIRECT YOUR PATH THE SOONER YOUR ARRIVAL TIME. Practice the skill of minimizing wasted motion in getting to the next position every time you move. Soon you will find yourself beating faster (but less efficient) opponents in the race to get to the next position!

PLOTTING YOUR NEXT MOVE: as much as we all aspire to have a high success rate for the performance of our favorite moves, the reality is that THE MAJORITY OF THE ATTEMPTED APPLICATIONS OF YOUR MOVES AGAINST SKILLED OPPONENTS WILL FAIL. That's the bad news. The good news is that the general slow pace of ground grappling means that in most cases YOU WILL KNOW WHEN THEY ARE LIKELY TO FAIL BEFORE THEY ACTUALLY DO. As a result, you can have a follow up move prepared to work even as the first fails. THIS IS THE TIME TO BE THINKING OF YOUR NEXT MOVE - BEFORE failure is complete, not AFTER. This will make you a dangerous combination fighter who can seamlessly go from attack to attack and ensnare even very good opponents, rather than a one shot at a time fighter who must rely on surprise or strength to catch people. Every time you find yourself on the cusp of failure with your moves, practice the mental skill of searching for an appropriate second attack BEFORE the total collapse of the first and watch your success rate double!

THE GREAT CHALLENGE OF OPEN GUARD -
reconciling your desire for offense with your
need for defense: Open guard play is probably
one of the most frustrating elements of Jiu Jitsu
for most players. It offers almost limitless
possibilities for attack with sweeps and
submissions, but it also offers our opponent
limitless opportunities for positional attacks of
his own - guard passes. As we are thinking about
our offensive possibilities it takes only a fraction
of a second for an opponent to blast past our
legs and in a flash we have gone from pondering
offense to scrambling desperately for defense
and preventing an opponent scoring with a
guard pass. Everything we do from open guard
has to be done with a sense of defensive
responsibility. The main thing that prevents an
opponent gaining the distance, angle and level
change he requires to get past our legs is our
connection to his body. If we are well connected
to him, we will follow his movement easily as he
tries to out flank our legs. If we lack sufficient

connection, he can pass your guard in a heartbeat and put you under great pressure. Whenever you begin to feel your connection to an opponent is failing, you must begin to shift from PULLING connection (offensive) to PUSHING connection (defensive) and thus create frames that prevents an opponent getting chest to chest contact and control of your head that will enable him to solidify a pass. Learning shift seamlessly from offensive grips to defensive frames as the second by second dynamic of the match unfolds is the key to reconciliation of your desire for offense and your need for defense from open guard.

FREAKING OUT ISN'T GOING TO HELP: It is natural when you find yourself in a bad situation in Jiu Jitsu to feel some degree of panic - no one likes losing, even in the gym, and so the intensity always goes up as the danger of losing increases. Now, as this feeling of foreboding starts to escalate into genuine concern, the danger of it degenerating into total panic increases. It's at this point that one starts to see chaos break out. Students will start exploding in various directions in order to affect a breakout. This can work in many cases at beginner level, since most beginners lack the ability to control and immobilize a wildly thrashing opponent. It can also work if you are bigger and stronger than an opponent. However, as size discrepancy decreases and skill levels rise, this will work less and less. If you were given a complex math problem, would it help you to solve it if you began by freaking out? No. In fact if we look at almost every daily problem we have to overcome, from flat tires, to navigating through an unfamiliar part of town, to paying bills over the phone, we see that it is almost never the case that wild emotional or physical reaction aid our ability to solve and overcome the problem. Jiu Jitsu is no different. Just as the solution to any complex math problem is best found with a calm mind that calmly and methodically searches for the solution, so too in Jiu Jitsu. Make your first reaction to a difficult hold in Jiu Jitsu be a grounding breath, and then a mental commitment to the idea of staying as calm as you can and THINKING your way out rather than FREAKING your way out. Look how calm Nicky Ryan as he works from a particularly tricky leg lock situation. This is the spirit you want to operate in whenever you find yourself on the defensive. This will ensure you prevail in all situations rather than just against smaller or less experienced opponents.

The majority of what we call elite performance is simply the degree to which some athletes take the fundamentals of our sport closer to the limits of their potential - the depth of your progress in Jiu Jitsu is entirely based upon the depth of your knowledge and the perfection of your expression of the fundamentals. Make the fundamentals your lifetime study and understand that you will never exhaust their potential even in ten lifetimes...

Printed in Great Britain
by Amazon